*The Smiles That Hid
The Sadness*

The Smiles That Hid The Sadness

Dee Kang

To Jessica

Best wishes

HPH Publishing
Chicago, IL

© 2007 Dee Kang. Printed and bound in Canada. All rights reserved. No part of this book may be reproduced or transmitted in any form or by any means, electronic or mechanical, including photocopying, recording, or by an information storage and retrieval system—except by a reviewer who may quote brief passages in a review to be printed in a magazine, newspaper, or on the web—without permission in writing from the publisher. For information, please contact HPH Publishing Inc., 333 West North Avenue, Chicago, IL 60610, USA.

Cover Illustration by Morgan Ramsdell, KoKo Mia Designs
Copyright: HPH Publishing Inc.

Although the author and publisher have made every effort to ensure the accuracy and completeness of information contained in this book, we assume no responsibility for errors, inaccuracies, omissions, or any inconsistency herein. Any slighting of people, places or organizations is unintentional. The persons mentioned in this book do not necessarily endorse the writing or content.

First printing 2007

ISBN 0-9776281-0-8
ISBN 13 9780977628100
LCCN: 2005937712

*This book
is dedicated to women in
suffering going through difficult
times in life*

Contents

Publisher's Note   ix

When I Ate, I Cried   1

Finding My Way In The World   33

Living The American Dream   49

Surviving The American Nightmare   81

The Sadness Flows Like Wine   141

We Endure Sadness To Know Happiness   165

Photographs   173

Publisher's Note

This is a highly personal and important journey. It was translated into prose by John Holt Sagan, a writer for HPH Publishing Inc., through recorded transcripts of interviews between Dee Kang and myself. I, like many in the Lincoln Park area of Chicago, have been a loyal Dee's customer for almost twenty years. It is my honor to be able to share this story with you.

In the writing of this book, we wanted you to hear the story as only Dee can tell it. Her English is not perfect, and she often speaks in the present tense. We believe this is part of the charm that is Dee Kang. To be true to her voice, at times, we have elected not to change the tense or grammatical incorrectness of the statement so you can hear the words in the way Dee would have spoken them.

We know you will enjoy getting to know Dee, and her story will leave you with much to think about.

Franchee D. Harmon
Editor-in-Chief

*The Smiles That Hid
The Sadness*

INTRODUCTION

Every day, for 24 years, customers have come to my restaurant. I've always tried to be the first person they see when they arrive. They come here from many places and many walks of life, you know? And I like to think that they come to find a moment of happiness. So when they arrive, I always have a smile for them.

This is how it has been for most of my life, okay? I have always tried to create happiness. Mostly, this happiness was for others. I thought I could make my mother happy, my children happy, my husband happy, my brothers and sisters happy, and my customers happy. I believed that in the end when everyone else was happy, I would be happy, too. That was before the day I had to choose between my own happiness and everyone else's.

It was Wednesday: a very normal restaurant day. Emily was answering the phones while I was taking care of customers. Above the noise of the kitchen and the cash register, I could hear Emily say, "Robert Kang is not here." But the caller continued to talk to her. She listened attentively, and I began to wonder why. As the call continued, Emily's face changed. Hesitantly, she turned to me. "Dee, I think you should take this call."

Robert Kang was a name we did not speak at the restaurant. He is my ex-husband. But I knew from the look on Emily's face that I could not ignore the call. I took the phone.

"I am calling from the American Consulate in Japan," the man began. "We need to inform you that Robert Kang is in a coma in a hospital in Osaka. It is our understanding that he does not have family in Japan."

I needed to go there right away.

Two days later, I boarded a plane to Japan, but as I laid awake during the thirteen-hour flight, I questioned myself "why?" While I felt that I did not have an answer, God answered me. He told me I must get Robert. Defiantly, I thought to myself and said to God, "I don't want to bring Robert back." Again I asked, "Why should I?" Once again God replied, "Because you must." Though I am a true believer, I have never thought of God as speaking directly to me. On that day, He did. Reluctantly, and with a very heavy heart, I agreed to follow the path He had chosen for me.

Now as I look back, I can see that I found the courage to follow my path to happiness on the plane that day. From the day I was born, the journey along that path has never been easy, but today, because of my belief in God, I am happy and so is my family. This story shares how we came to live that happiness.

When I Ate, I Cried

It has become clear to me that my mom doesn't believe in happiness; that this is possible or a normal state of being. And from our earliest days, she tried to make us believe the same. I learned just how impossible my mom thought it was to achieve happiness when I was six years old.

Though we were very poor, not everyone in our village was. In fact, the family next to us had a very successful restaurant business. They were such a nice family, with the grandparents, parents, and a little daughter. I liked the daughter very much and tried to spend as much time with her as possible. Her family could afford to do many things that we could not do. Still, we played together and spent time together. Often I would go with her to piano lessons at a special place. You know, Chinese culture, and Asian culture in general, is very formal. So I was not allowed to go in while my friend took her lessons. But I would sit quietly on the single step outside and listen to the beautiful music. It was so wonderful to me. As I listened, I imagined her tiny fingers touching the keys as they made melodious tones. And silently, I longed to be able to go inside to play, too.

One day, we walked home together, talking excitedly about the day and her lesson. When I got into the house, I rushed over to my mom and said, "Mom, I really want to take piano lessons." My mother looked at me as if I had just said I wanted to reach the stars. She grabbed me firmly by the arm, dragged me across the room, and out into the street. Angrily, she pointed to the moon and said, "If you can reach the moon, you can have piano lessons."

I didn't know it then, but I would spend most of my life trying to prove to my mother that you can reach the moon and have happiness.

Growing up in poverty is never easy. The Chinese who were born in Korea—like other migrants throughout history forced to leave their homeland or die—we suffered a lot. I am the third child in my family, born in the year of the Rooster, 1957.

On the day I was born, there was no joy. I was a girl. My father did not even want to name me. He gave in only after protests from my grandma. "You have to at least give her a name," she pleaded. So I was called, "Lian Dee." Lian means to connect to a brother. It was my father's way of saying that I must bring a son to our family. Not only did I bring one son, I brought three. Two survived.

I also have one sister and an older brother. My oldest brother is from my mother's first marriage. Her first husband died tragically at the beginning of the Korean War. While his death pushed my family into poverty, it allowed me to be born. The creation of my life is an example of how God gives and He takes. It is one of the most natural aspects of how balance is maintained in the world.

My sister was the first child between my mother and father, you know, so the first child between the two of them was a girl, but that was okay. And they had a little money at that time, so they could make a living. My father was working at a winemaking company, brewing a special type of rice wine that Korean people like to drink. Very strong wine, okay? My father was sort of, like, working at the factory.

The day I was born my father went out gambling after he found out that I was a girl. He would not give my mom anything to eat. He didn't cook anything. He swore at her, you know, and said some stupid things, because I was a girl. Finally, he just left.

My grandma had to deliver me, because I couldn't wait. In

those times, you didn't go to the hospital to give birth, there was a woman who came to your house when your wife was ready to give birth, a midwife. But I came out before she arrived, so my grandma delivered me, and waited for the midwife to cut the cord. My grandma was scared to cut the cord, so she stood there holding me, waiting.

Though my Mom does not believe in happiness and often did not show love, my grandma and other people gave me strong examples that this is possible.

My grandpa passed away when I was five, so my mom had to go to my grandma. My youngest brother was a year old, and my mom still had to breast-feed him, so she had to take him and go quickly. I stayed with my Mom as she hurried to get her things, and then went out to the street to see her leave. To my surprise, oh my God! There was a cab outside. I hadn't known they were going to take a cab! For the first time in our life, in our family, somebody was getting to take a car trip, getting into the cab to go somewhere. Oh my goodness, this was huge, big news! I was pretty brave, since I was young: I ran to the cab and said, "No, no, no! I want to get in. I want to see how it feels to sit in the car!"

The cab wanted to leave, and my mom said, "No, no," I couldn't go, but I wouldn't let go of the cab. I held on as tightly as I could, so finally my mom had no choice but to take me, and I went to my grandma's house.

After the funeral was over, my mom left me there because my grandma was scared of only one thing: ghosts. My grandma was not scared of anything. She wasn't scared of mice. She wasn't scared of rats. Nothing. Except dead people.

Back then, when people died, they didn't go to a funeral home. The body was just in your living room. For three days. Okay? So for three days, my grandpa laid there covered with a white shroud, but I was young, so I didn't get scared.

My mom had to return to take care of the family, so she left me there to take care of grandma. One of the few nice things my mom says about me is that I am a very good listener, even at that age, and a very well behaved person, which is perhaps why my grandma loved me so. And her love gave me a taste of the love, which ran short at home.

Imagine the loyalty of a beloved granddaughter: if my grandma goes to bathroom...I follow her. If my grandma goes out...I follow her. If she had gone to the moon, I would have followed her there, too.

In those times, they made funerals into visual ceremonies. They put the casket outside. Then they used colored paper to make a lot of horses, houses, people, and money to burn at the cemetery for the use of the deceased in heaven. They told me, "Now they have a house, a horse to ride, money to use up there." The little people were burned, too, and as I watched the little people burning, they said, "And then they have everybody to take care of them."

I loved to see that! When I was little, I loved to see that...

After the funeral, I stayed with my grandma for a long time, because I didn't have to go to school. When I left my grandma's house, she bought me a sweater, a pink sweater with just a little blue on it. Not only was that my first sweater, but the first article of new clothing I had in my life! I remember wearing that sweater for a huge long time. When threads tore out here and there, my mom would open up the weave and put them back together.

I am one of those people who is a nurturer by instinct. From the time my youngest brother was born, I took care of him. I also took care of other children as well. I think it was God's way of blessing me, because babysitting is one thing I really did well.

In the countryside, we had a Chinese church. Our pastor and pastor's wife had two children (I don't remember if the girl or boy was first), but the second child had a disability. I think it was polio.

So they were praying every single day, day and night, they were praying for this child.

Personally, I loved to go to church, because at church they gave you a crayon to use, and paper to cut out with scissors. And then, once in a while, they gave you one or two candies, and then also, once or twice a day, they would give you a cookie. But I loved coloring most of all, and then you could cut something! We didn't have that at home. We didn't have crayons at home. The only way we could use those materials was to go to the church, and every time I went to church, I took my youngest brother. We just stayed in the church.

When I was little, I stayed in the church, always listening, always listening, so my ear has all those beats and rhythms. That's how I learned to sing church songs.

I was so good at doing work for the pastor and his wife, which made me feel good about myself, and, besides that, I didn't even want to go home after I finished school, because at home I didn't have anything.

After school, I went directly to the church, and they welcomed me, and loved me, because of why? I was such a good worker!

During prayer, okay, I had their child on my back, held in place with a Korean swaddling cloth like a wrapped-up bed sheet.

I would wash the rice for dinner for them, making sure to add water up to my palm, as my Mom taught me to do, and then cook it. Sometimes, while the rice was cooking, I would sweep the floor and wash the baby's diapers, and then hang up everything.

I enjoyed making one part of the world clean and pleasant, and I enjoyed feeling like my work would prove to someone like my mother that I could do those chores without despair.

By the time they finished the prayers, the rice was ready, but I would never eat there. I handed over the rice to them, I handed over the baby, and then I went home. I did that for a long time, and I never asked for anything back. I just loved to do it. I was so happy to go there after school because I felt like there was love there.

The pastor and his wife were contracted to be in Korea only

for a certain period of time. I think it was two years. After their contract was up, they had to go back to Taiwan. I was so sad to see them leave. The day before they left I came to their house like normal, you know? I do all the chores and take care of the baby. I want to do an extra special job, because I know they are leaving and doing a really good job for them eased my sadness. Once I had finished all of my chores, I went to the pastor and his wife and said, "I'm finished now. I go home." The pastor and wife asked me to come over to them, and I noticed that they have a little package in their hand. "This is for you, Dee," they said, smiling. Oh my God! I opened the package and screamed, "It's a backpack. My very own backpack!" I was so excited. I hugged them so tightly. I was so happy.

Before the pastor and his wife had given me this new backpack, my mom had made my backpack from a sack: the sacks that would hold the flour. She would boil the bag then add soap to get the letters off and to make it whiter. After it dried, she would hold it together to make a sack by sewing some string to the edges. Like everything else that I had as a child, my mom sewed it together to make something old into something new for me.

That is the way it was. Except the sweater from my grandma, I never had new things, including clothes, which had been bought from a store. I always got the things my sister left to me, as altered by my mother.

I remember starting first grade. My mom kind of altered one of my sister's red skirts to fit me. At that time I was still smaller than my sister, so my mom kind of altered the bottom by folding it inside and sewing it. When I wore that red skirt, I knew everybody else had new clothes to go to school. But I did not.

During school, the children all played at the playground without the toys and equipment we see in the United States. All they would do is play double-dutch, one person turning each side of a big jump rope for the people jumping in and out. They shot rubber bands; they played with a ball. That's all we children had. At school that day, everyone else was playing, but I hung back, feeling ashamed because I thought I was the only one who didn't have a new outfit. That was my first day of school. I remember I didn't go to the playground the whole time. I was just at the school entrance by myself, sitting there because I was scared that people would see that I wore my sister's skirt.

I lived with that shame for a very long time.

We celebrated Chinese New Year in the traditional way. We had to cook a lot, even if we were poor. We borrowed money and started preparing a month ahead of time. We didn't have a refrigerator, but it was cold outside, so that is where we stored the special foods we made. We had red bean paste for stuffing steamed buns and making designs on bread. It was too overwhelming for one person to do, so if one family was cooking, my mother would go there to help, and then to another family's the next day, and so did all the other Chinese mothers in the month before New Year, taking turns and keeping on top of which house needed to do what on which day.

You had to be very careful what you said. You could not say something unlucky around Chinese New Year, something that would bring bad luck.

We also had to do a big cleaning before the New Year. After the New Year, my mom would hide the broom, because of the risk of sweeping good luck away, but before the New Year, we had to clean every corner, even the corners inside drawers and boxes.

One time, I remember my mom was helping this family with the cooking and my sister broke one of the bowl covers with a loud crash. Of course, my mom said, "Sorry, sorry, kids don't know what they're doing, do they? It was an accident." But oh my God, after we got home, she went totally nuts.

She punished my sister, my two brothers, and me so bad. Oh my God, I can still remember that it was so bad.

And one time, at home on New Year's Eve, we had dumplings boiling in water, with their light, delicate skin so easily broken, and I had trouble remembering that you cannot say an unlucky thing like, "It's broken!" That would be bad luck. You have to say something to creatively indicate what happened, like "Oh, my goodness, look at this! It's so over money! It's going to blow all the money in the house away!" I didn't think to say it any other way but "Oh my god! This dumpling is broken!" And my mom hit me so bad. She sometimes used a broom, sometimes a wooden stick, and sometimes—this hurt the most—she used something metal.

At that time in Korea, nobody had gas stoves and heaters. We burned charcoal, heaps of it, in four-legged fireplaces. My mother was not above beating us with a heavy little bar of iron that plugged up the hole at the bottom of the fire. It left black soot-marks on our skin, which turned blue from deep bruising in the same places within a day. It hurt so much, and she used it the most.

My mother's money was always short, as short as her temper, and she saved on fuel by purchasing our charcoal in bulk. She gave it a special storage room, and it witnessed our punishments, for she had gotten into the habit of beating us right there, away from the rest of the house. You needed massive amounts of charcoal to get through the winter, and even in summertime, you needed plentiful charcoal for cooking, and it seemed that my mother's need to beat us was just as close to inexhaustible as the coal and darkness in that room.

When my mom would get upset, even when we didn't do anything bad—and we really didn't do anything that bad—she punished us in the little room, all together, my sister, my two little brothers, and me.

First, she would hit us. After that, we had to stand up in the little room full of charcoal.

It was so black. It was so dark, as dark as the words "no electricity," and rats ran all over. I was scared of rats because I had already been bitten once. Oh my god, I cried so bad.

Next to the storage room was the bathroom. In those old times, we didn't have a flush toilet, of course. It was a hole, one little hole above a water tank, and it smelled so bad that going to the bathroom was the next scariest thing to being locked in the dark with the rats. I'm sorry to talk about it, but when the toilet tank was kind of full, you had to pull on the top so it could protect you from the pee surging up.

Ironically, if the collection workers had come and cleaned the barrel on one of those rare occasions, had come and taken the poo, but still left some water inside, we would go there to have bowel movements and nearly drown in the backsplash. The water came up, and not just the water, the pee, the poop, whatever was there.

The cleaning crews sometimes came three times a year, but often we were lucky if they came once, and it smelled so bad, but if you didn't touch anything, it was okay. It is amazing that we didn't get infections, but I remember getting none, zero.

And you know what? We didn't have toilet paper. We used newspaper, and the old-time newspaper was all black, so you would be black everywhere. My hands were always black. It was not like now, when we go to the bathroom, then wash our hands with soap. We didn't wash our hands because we didn't have water. Every drip, every drop, every drip of water was precious.

In fact, everything was. We didn't waste anything. When we were eating, we could not leave one grain of rice in the bowl. If we did, oh, you watch, my mom could really get pissed off. When we were little kids, it was hard to pick at every grain with our chopsticks, but we tried. Our family's goal was to end up with nothing to throw away. There was no garbage, because everything that could go to our stomachs went. Even things that kind of smelled bad. She would wash suspicious food, really soak it in water, then cook it, boil it again, and we would eat it. We didn't get sick. Maybe we weren't allowed to get sick.

I never ate beef when I was little, because any beef we could afford was placed before my father and two younger brothers. Even today, I'm not crazy about beef. I love seafood because we lived by the ocean, and as poor people we could wade in the wet sand with a container and hoe for the clams. I did that a lot.

My father would measure the rice. For us, you know, rice is very important. We have to eat rice every day, you know? It's like bread for Americans, or flour. Every day, for dinner, we had rice.

Say my mom would take the rice back to our house. My father would measure it. Then my father would go out gambling, lose money, come home, and be hitting my mother.

All this anger at my mom, and if my father would go out and win money, he would buy opium, come home, and smoke.

At the time, my brother was little, so you know what? He tried to grab the opium one time. Maybe he would have put it in his mouth, which could have killed him. My father burned him with his opium pipe, so my brother would be too scared to ever touch the opium again. This is what I heard from my mom, okay?

I don't remember much from when I was a baby, obviously, but what I can remember is my father. He was like a king. Whatever he wanted to do, he did.

He went out and fooled around. He went out to smoke opium. He went out to gamble for many days. He didn't come home.

When he came home, my mom was just like a mouse that saw a cat. She had to hide, okay? She had to hide, because she was so scared that he would hit her.

And he would. Serious hitting. And like a mouse that saw a cat, mom just didn't know where to go, you know? And even though he went out and did all these bad things, and came home and hit her, my mom had to treat him like a king, okay?

The way he treated my mom taught me that a woman was just like nothing, you know? So I never thought I had a father's love. I didn't know what love from a father was. Love from a male? All I know is, my mom looked at my father like a mouse looks at a cat. Later after I married, it was exactly the same way for me, too.

By the time I had reached third grade, our family struggles began to get really tough. The Korean president had changed. It had been Dr. Lee, but he passed away, and they elected a new president. When the new president came in, he knew a lot of people were drug addicts, so the minute he became president, he put all of the drug people in jail, including my father.

My mother didn't have any skills, you know? The whole Korea was so poor that there were not even people who would hire her as a maid, or anything. Even if she was hired as a maid, we children were too little for her to go out to work.

My grandma opened the way to a little food for us, because at that time my mom's one younger sister got married to rich people, so my grandma could supply us with a little rice and a little flour.

So when I was in third grade, I had to go work for a cousin of my father who had a lot of money and lived in the same town as us. In those old times, people didn't have washing machines or anything. I would go to their house to sweep, mop the floor, and do the laundry by hand. After all of that, I would wash the rice, draw the rice water, and cook the rice for their dinner for them. They would cook other things, and after they finished eating, I would wash all the dishes. You think I made money? No. I would get one meal, okay?

As I ate the meal, I would cry, because I knew my brothers were at home having nothing to eat. Nowadays you get a lot of plastic forks and plastic containers, but at that time, the whole Korea was kind of poor, because of the aftermath of the war, you know? So you couldn't say, "Can I bring this home for my brother?" There was no way, so all I did was eat for myself. I had to. So every time I ate, I cried because I knew my brothers were at home suffering.

I think my father had been in jail for a little over a year when the whole community of Chinese people in our little city, our little village came up with the money to bail my father out. Those were nice people.

So my father came out. And I remember that day as the one day I went home and immediately thought, "Oh my gosh, we have something to eat!" The smell of meat cooking, the smell of shrimp cooking, I guessed, was so good! I saw, "My mom is cooking!" You know? "My God," I said, "something is going on!" I was a little girl, you know? Something WAS going on, indeed: I found out my father was coming home.

My father coming out of jail was like a king coming home, just like a king who went out to fight in a war coming home. My mom cooked the best meal for him, and he didn't ask, "Do you guys want to eat or not?" He ate alone, and after he ate, he went out.

Whatever my father had left over, it went to my two brothers. After my two brothers, the food went to my sister. Then it came to me. If I had a little left, I gave it to my mom. My mom was always the last one. You know, I don't know how many meals she suffered without. She was always the one who came after the last one. Everything we had was for the use and benefit of my father first. My father was the king, after my father came the boys, then it was the girls, and after the girls, my mom, and that was the order.

I remember that, after my father came out, his addiction didn't stop. He was still doing drugs. I didn't see him doing drugs, but I knew.

Anyway, after he got out of jail, my parents opened a restaurant in the front of the house, but my father was not working, not steadily. He went on benders smoking opium. That had always been the problem. He just came home to take the money away, and sometimes we didn't see him for weeks.

One day a group of people came in. They all looked ugly, with swollen faces, and they all wore white gowns and white sashes tied around their heads, and they all had canes. They started talking to my mom, asking where my father was.

"I don't know. If you know where he is, I want to go find him myself. I'm sorry," my mom said.

"Your husband owes me money. You give it to me."

"I don't have money for you, okay? Do you know I don't even have money to feed the kids?"

Then they started hitting my mom. I was so scared that I hid under the table. I couldn't protect my mom. My mom had a bloody nose. She cried, and as she cried, she cursed at them. They broke a table; they broke the telephone; they used the canes to break the whole front of the house.

After they were gone, I asked, "Mom, how much did we owe them?"

"The money your daddy owes them, in a lifetime we cannot pay them back."

Now that I am an adult, I try to tell my mom she said things like that, but she doesn't remember, or won't.

I was in the fourth grade, but I said to myself, "I'm going to make money when I grow up. I don't care how I will make money, but I'm going to make money. I'm going to make my mom happy. I'm going to take care of my mom."

I was always the sensitive one. I never let my mom open her mouth to say, "Dee, can you help me with this or that?" I only considered myself truly helpful if before my mom asked, I had already helped her.

On the other hand, by the time my mom opened her mouth, she was already pretty mad, so we all had to be very sensible of what she might want.

Those were tough times, but there were also good times. We didn't have any toys, but I'd round up my two brothers, and we'd go to the mountain to catch butterflies and climb. We kind of smashed some of the butterflies in the pages of a book, to preserve them. In the fall, we would pick up the nice leaves and put them in a book, and say, "This leaf will make you smart, that leaf will make you healthy."

If you opened out our book, we had all these leaves and butterflies.

We played with beanbags a lot, or the equivalent, since we didn't have beans. We put sand inside, and threw the beanbag, and if it touched somebody, they were out.

I was so good at the jump rope, and playing with a ball, because I was a tomboy.

We played a game called five stone, something like the American children's game of jacks, with stones we picked up from the street. I was so good at that.

I don't like to lose, you know? Since I was little, I haven't liked losing.

I loved the holiday we called "Double Ten," October 10, when the whole school had a running tournament in celebration of the founding of the Democratic Republic of Taiwan. We didn't have running shoes, so my mom used the same sacks my backpack was made out of to make me running slippers to protect my feet.

When I ran, I was always in first place, so I got to line up with the other winners for prize pencil sharpeners, erasers, and other rewards, which I proudly treasured.

The Taiwanese government supported the school's Double Ten celebration, and the winning got me a lot of supplies that lasted for a long time.

We went to Chinese school, so we had to pay tuition. Even the Korean children had to pay money for school, which was a social problem, since many families knew they would never be able to afford it. With the father I had, we certainly never had the money to pay tuition, but the administrators of the Chinese school were nice. They just let us go, go, go, finally coming to my sister's sixth grade graduation day, the culmination of our six-year grammar school.

My sister had to participate in graduation, and, as an important part of that, you had to take a picture with your diploma. There was a crisis: they wouldn't give my sister a diploma because we owed so much money. I was so happy to see my sister graduate, but then I wondered why she didn't have a diploma to hold so she could take a diploma picture. My brother said, "We owe the school money." I had not known that.

And then the principal was so nice. He said, "Just let her take a picture with somebody's diploma," so I think she did, a little later on. They made an issue out of it, though, holding a meeting and everything, before they finally let my sister hold that substitute diploma, and after the picture was over, they took it away promptly. This is how I remember my sister graduating sixth grade, okay?

I can't really recall my oldest brother ever living with us. I don't know when he left home, but I think it was when I was in third grade. How he left home and where he went, I didn't know, but my brother was a lot like his father, smart and adventurous. And his creative ideas helped save our family. The death of his father was very tragic, and sometimes, I feel that mom still carries this loss with her.

My grandma's mother couldn't support her kids, either, you know? When it was grandfather's turn to get a wife, my grandma was given to him. They got married and had children, and my mom was the oldest.

Grandfather was a bookkeeper. He spoke really good Japanese. He was doing bookkeeping in Korea for a company that sold fabric.

My mom and grandma lived in the Shandong region of China while my grandpa often lived in Korea. It was very easy to get from the Shandong region of China to Korea by boat. So many Chinese did this. Especially during times of strife, economic necessity, or when other countries were being aggressive.

At the time my grandpa was working in Korea, the Japanese were starting to come into China, controlling the country and killing people. If you didn't listen, they would kill you. They sexually molested the girls and women; they took whatever they wanted.

So my grandma and mom got really scared. My mom told me she would see a dead body lying in the street, and Japanese soldiers passing, and even though the person was already dead, they used the bayonet knives on the ends of their rifles to stab the dead body again. My mom was so scared of that. She was just six years old. Finally, my grandfather said, "Why don't you guys come to Korea, okay? Maybe it's a little safer." My grandma and my mom took a huge ship and went to Korea. They thought they could have peace there.

But there were Japanese soldiers in Korea, too. So the first thing they saw after the long ride on the ship was a Japanese soldier in the Korean port. There was a cow passing by the Japanese soldier's car, okay? The cow didn't know how to stop, so it pulled right in front and soldier's car had to stop. The soldier was angry. He got out of the car and used the same weapon my mother had learned to be afraid of in China—the rifle with the sharp knife in the front—to kill the cow. That's the first thing my mom got out of Korea, the first thing she saw.

But anyway, at least they had my grandpa there, you know? After they moved to Korea, my grandmother had four more children, two girls and two boys.

My mom was the only one born in China. Because she was the oldest she didn't have a lot of education. Her job was to take care of her brothers and sisters. When she went to Korea, she had to learn Japanese, because the Japanese controlled Korea at that time. Everybody had to be educated in Japanese. But she only went for a very short period of time, and then, because she had four siblings and they were really poor, she had to take care of them. So my mom was the one who had to suffer.

My grandfather, like a lot of Chinese people who went to Korea, found a job, and sent money home. It was better than staying in China. Many of the Chinese people owned fabric stores, and there was even a special name for Chinese people. My grandfather didn't own a fabric store; he did bookkeeping for one. He was a very honest person, and the store owner didn't take care of a lot of things. With all the care my grandpa took, he was like a second boss there. He had started really young, and they had trained him well for his responsibilities.

My mom was the only one in her family who didn't have a lot of education. She had to stay home, take care of four siblings, cook, and clean. If my mom didn't do that, my grandma would get angry. If my mom snuck out to go to school, when she came back, my grandma would tear up all her books. She would say, "Girls, what do you need to study for? Just stay home and do jobs for me. Do the housework for me. That's all you need to do. And what do you need to study for? What is the useful purpose of that?"

So my grandma was really, really strict, because all she wanted my mom to be was like a slave. But my mom managed to learn a little bit. She doesn't know a lot of the Chinese characters, which are hard to learn because some characters have the same sound and different meanings, but she knows a few. When we were overseas, and she wrote us letters, we would have to read them over and over again to finally understand her meaning, because she only used one pronunciation for everything. We had to guess a lot of the time.

But my mother got married at seventeen, okay, to this very nice man, this very, very smart, handsome man. He owned a big, huge restaurant in the countryside. And after she got married, from what I heard, her husband was a really, really nice person. Young, handsome, very smart. At age nineteen, she gave birth to my oldest brother.

After his birth, my mother's first husband wanted to go back to

China, just to show, "Hey, I have a son!" Just to kind of show off, I guess. A lot of people told him not to go, because all of the Chinese people staying in Korea didn't have Korean citizenship. We were still Chinese, so we had to have something similar to the green card foreigners need to work in the United States today. And at that time, Korea was not stable. The Korean War hadn't started, but the undertones that led to the war were emerging.

All of his family said, "Don't go. This is not a good time to go!" But he didn't listen. Then people told him, "If you go, you better come back in three months. You have a brand-new son." And he said, "Okay," so they let him leave.

He didn't come back in three months. He didn't come back in six months. He came back a year later. So by the time he came back, Korea was already at a high peak of tension. Any day, the war was going to be starting.

Because he was so smart, my mom's first husband spoke perfect Korean and Chinese. A lot of Chinese people living in Korea spoke very broken Korean, because they weren't born there, but somehow he spoke fluent Korean and fluent Chinese. When he came back, there was already a Korean spy starting to follow him. They thought, "Why were you in China for that long? There's got to be something you're doing." So once he arrived in the Korean port, coming by ship, the secret police were on his tail.

He knew that they were following him, so he didn't go home right away. Instead, he went to a little Korean city.

Somehow, my mom found out he had come back, so she went there to meet him. After they met, he said he was not going to go home, because he had these feelings that somebody had followed him. He told my mom to go home, however.

The minute my mom left, he got arrested and put in jail. At the local jails, which this was, if you went and gave money, you could get out, so my mom gave money to this man, her husband's father's brother or some relative of hers, but this guy was a gambling person. On the way to bail my mom's first husband out, he gambled all the money and lost it.

Now, the possibility of the war starting was getting very high, and the authorities transferred him from the small jail to the big jail, which was far away.

Once you transfer to the big jail, it's hard to get out, so by the time my mom found out he had been transferred, he was already in the big jail, and then the Korean War started. My mom had my brother to take care of—he was a little over a year old—but she also had my uncle—her own baby brother—to take care of as a favor to her mother. He was a little over two years old.

North Korea had now come into the South. It was getting very, very serious. There were tunnels in the mountains, and you had to hide in them during the day and sneak out only at night. And they had these little dynamites that they dropped from airplanes, made like a candy wrapper, or just like a daisy. Once you touched it, if the kids touched it, it blew up, you know? So my mom had to put my brother on her back and hold my uncle's hands. She told him, "Don't ever, ever touch anything," and my uncle really listened good, so he didn't touch anything, but those dynamites were all over. You had to be really careful not to step on them, you know? With the two children, using the tunnels in the mountains, my mom made her way to the big city to see her husband in the jail.

By this time, the South Koreans had found out that the North Koreans were coming. The prison guards had been nasty to the prisoners when they first put them in jail. So they thought that when they got out, they would kill their captors. Thinking ahead, they ordered a big truck. Then they put the prisoners into the truck, and took them to the mountains. They made the prisoners dig a big hole and later lined everybody up. Then they shot them, just bang, bang, bang, you know?

My mom was a couple miles away, on her way there when it happened. By the time she got there, they had killed everybody. All she found were the holes they had been buried in. That's how my mom's first husband died.

Then, finally, the war was over. The Korean War was very short. My mother had nowhere to go because she had been so scared of the North Korean and Chinese army during the war—the Chinese army was helping North Korea, too, and they would come into the restaurant, asking for food to eat. They killed a cow, you know, so my mom worried that they would kill her, too, and they would just ask for things, ask for anything, and they lived in the house and at the restaurant. My mother got so scared of them.

After the war was over, she took my brother and uncle back home to my grandma's. Well, my grandma's home was still really, really poor. They couldn't even survive themselves, and here were my mom and her son.

At that time, my father, who was my mother's second husband, snuck from China to Korea. My father came to Korea much later on when the communists' starting to get strong in China during China's civil war. All the junkies had to go to Taiwan. Then the Maoist started to get very strong, so my father got out of China.

When my father went to Korea, he went to the small city where my mom's family lived. This one family with the same last name as us said: "You know, our relative"—meaning my father—"has a lot of money, and he's handsome…" My father WAS handsome! "Even though you guys are twelve years different in age…" My mom was only twenty-two, so my father must have been thirty-four years old.

My grandma heard that my father had a lot of money, so she just told my mom to go to him. It wasn't even that she told my mother to marry my father, particularly—"Just go to him, because at least you won't have to suffer." That's how my mom and my father got together, okay?

So after they got together…I mean, my mom had already had one marriage, and it was really not my mom's fault how her husband had passed—by getting killed—but people just thought, "There you go, getting married again. You're not pure anymore!" They were really mean.

After my mom married my father, and they were living together, she found out my father was a drug addict. She also found out my father was fooling around with other women because he was so handsome. She found out my father was gambling, too. The only thing my father was not doing was drinking. He didn't drink because his body could not take alcohol. Other than that, women, opium, gambling, you name it. He did everything.

He had a little money, okay? But here's what that meant: he snuck to Korea with one of his far cousins—the cousin I went to work for when my father was in jail. The matchmaker, the person who had the same last name as us said: "They have so much money!" She said my father had so much money, the boat almost turned upside down, but later my mom found out that was not true. All the money was his cousin's money, not my father's money.

So, for us it was a good thing that my oldest brother was like his father, not mine. When I came to fifth grade, I came back from school one day, and my mom said, "We all have to move to Seoul, because your brother is going to open a restaurant, and we are all going to live there."

My brother had been kind of lost, never growing up with us, living in Seoul, the capital city, while we lived in the countryside. All that time, all my life, he was going to school there and working part-time at a restaurant right outside the campus building.

He was a very smart guy, very, very smart. He was very capable of working, studying, and doing everything he wished.

So he was kind of supporting himself, then he lived in the restaurant, but now the owner could not keep him on due to a change in his situation. My brother, in his first year of high school, built his own restaurant out of bricks, without a building license or anything, okay?

He built, like, a warehouse, and put a roof on top, and opened a noodle house especially for the students to come to eat noodles at lunchtime.

We moved to Seoul so my mom and dad could work there, and I resumed the sixth grade at the grammar school in our new neighborhood.

When I was in the countryside, I went to school and studied really hard because I didn't want to make any trouble for my mom. She suffered so much, my brothers and I felt, that we could not allow her to suffer anything we could prevent.

I studied so well at that country school, but every time grades came out, no matter how hard I tried, I was always in the third place. At that time, they gave us rankings as first, second, third place, rather than the American grades of A, B, C, D, or saying "you're in the top five percent." One time, after I took a test, I was sure I had one hundred percent, but when the report card came out, my work had once again placed me no higher than third. Always! So many years, for all of grammar school, really, had been like this. I knew there had to be something unfair going on.

Later, I found out that the principal's daughter and teacher's sister were in the same class as I was, so the principal's daughter was always in first place and the teacher's sister in second.

But people in my family knew I really studied hard.

The school in Seoul was much bigger, so it made sense that I only made sixth place in the class on our first test. Still, my parents were angry that the new school was forcing me to repeat sixth grade. They also felt they were being asked to spend too much money on school supplies.

At Seoul, students were expected to use a ballpoint pen to ink our assignments. I couldn't afford even that, and I yearned to return to the countryside, where inexpensive golf pencils had been considered adequate for schoolwork, so that every student could rely on the school to provide this most important tool for learning.

We used those pencils all the way to the end.

One day, arriving at the big school without my ink pen, I sat outside the building, weeping again. Suddenly my brother passed by, doing a delivery.

"Why are you crying?" He asked.

"I didn't have a ballpoint pen. Everybody else is using a ballpoint pen, and I feel so ashamed of not having it."

"Ah, don't go anywhere. Stay right here!"

He came back and, in a moment I'll never forget, handed me a ballpoint pen. That's my brother!

His instant noodle restaurant opened with no electricity and no water. In the entire neighborhood, in fact, the school was the only building that had electricity, except a few private homes. Every morning, two times a morning, my sister had to go almost a mile to fetch the water the restaurant needed, carrying it on her shoulders in two big buckets. My brother needed the huge water tank at the restaurant to be full. I survived the launch of my brother's restaurant unscathed, because I was two years younger than my sister, and a schoolgirl, but my sister, my younger brother, my mom, and my father all helped.

Yes, even my father helped. He couldn't do drugs by that time, in Seoul, due to the changing times, but his attitude was still bad. We were still all scared of him...

I think all of my sister's hard work in those days is the reason she isn't as tall as the rest of the family. She carried that crushingly heavy water right at the time she was supposed to grow, and we didn't have any short family that I can think of.

Anyway, I stayed in school as the restaurant opened, and I didn't help a lot. Actually, I didn't spend much time at home, either, preferring to hole up in the dorms with the boarding students. Our family, once again, had enough to eat, since food was our stock in trade, but we still didn't have a lot of money. We could not really afford to light up the house at night, and my eyes were getting bad as it was.

In class, I could not see the writing on the board. The teacher put me in the front row to help me, which was embarrassing. That wasn't nice in a coed school, to be tall and always sitting all the way in the front. They made fun of me, you know?

Still I never told my mom, "My eyes are bad, please give me glasses." Because I knew she could not afford it. If I asked, it would only give her more trouble. I knew it was just too much for them to do that.

Instead of troubling my mother, I sat in the front row and endured the bad eyesight all the way from junior high school to the third year of high school, when I finally got glasses. Even today, I kind of look at people blindly sometimes, and I think it's because I kept quiet for so long.

My sister's short stature and my bad eyesight are just two examples of the permanent damage wrought by our approach to our mother and hers to us—although our mother could probably show her hair graying at forty and the lifeless thumb of her left hand to attest to her own debilitations resulting from motherhood.

Anyway, later on, the restaurant had to be closed down, because it was an illegal building. They came and locked the doors with big padlocks.

My brother had stopped going to school while he was opening the restaurant, and chosen to keep working there daily rather than resume his classes, because he was banking on his intelligence and aptitude for independent study, plus the letter, or perhaps the spirit, of the school rules, to allow him to graduate provided that he still did well on his final exam. When the test date came, he did manage to go and take it, and his exam came out perfect. Perfect! But the school wouldn't give him a break. They wouldn't let him graduate because he didn't go to classes—even though he scored high, even though he passed the test.

With the restaurant shut down by the authorities, what were

we going to do?

My mom went back to the countryside. We still had the house there, after all. My younger brother and I stayed at the dorm in Seoul, and my father went back to working at the factory as a winemaker. This reversal of fortune is the reason my sister didn't go to high school.

It turned out that my brother had no choice but to transfer to another, and smaller, high school in a different city, which would allow him to attend just the third year in high school so he could gain the Chinese high school diploma that would allow him to take some kind of test to come to America, which was his dream.

You had to take the TOEFL test to get into American universities. And to take the TOEFL, you had to have a high school diploma.

This second, countryside high school was near the second biggest city in Korea, and after a year of study, and acing the TOEFL, my brother got into university in the United States. It was huge, huge, big news in the little countryside, because at that time, if you went to America, it was like you were going to the moon.

So my brother went to America. I was so proud of that because only two people had gone to America in the surrounding country in the year my brother left; the matchmaker's son had gone the year before.

All of a sudden, my family attained a new status. It wasn't that we felt like celebrities, but we seemed to think, "Oh, now we can look at people." Now we can walk with pride, heads up. Before it was always like we were second-class, even if we children hadn't done anything wrong.

Once he was in America, my brother sent money home to deepen the improvement in our respectability. He would regularly stash 100 US dollars in between the film and black plastic backing of the normal-looking Polaroid instant snapshots enclosed in his letters. In Korea, we could survive so many, many months on that much money. We so looked forward to his letters, and we became ecstatic when we saw one had a picture inside.

Our situation got a lot better. We still weren't rich, in fact we were still just barely making a living, but we could eat. We still couldn't ask for a lot of things, like new clothes or something, but we could go to school full and eat two more meals for a total of three meals a day, and my two younger brothers were able to join me at the dorm, which was lucky because the countryside still didn't have a high school or junior high.

One Sunday, I woke up in our fourth floor dorm room surrounded by girls crowding to see out the window, which looked out towards the mountains. I tried to see what they were looking at, but I couldn't tell what was going on. Later, I found out that a neighbor boy had been electrocuted trying to steal electricity from the wires on top of our wooden power poles. He had climbed up and gotten stuck, and the sparks had ignited his body, and everyone watched him burn.

The fire truck was there, but the house whose power he had been trying to divert was right on the side of the mountain in a steep spot, and they couldn't do anything. Even if it was my first year of high school, we were little girls seeing this terrible thing. Some girls could even see the oil dripping down as his human fat burned like fuel. That is what life was like back then.

Throughout my high school years, I always felt low self-esteem because we were so poor. I never had dreams of going to college or something. All I wanted to do was keep my promise of making my mom happy by making money.

So in the third year, while everyone was taking tests to go to Taiwan to continue their studies, I thought about how I could make money, to make my mom happy. Over and over and over, I asked myself the same questions: "How could I make money to change the situation of my family? How could I make enough money so my mom and father would not fight a lot? How can I make money so there will be no more family grief?"

I was going to change our situation, and I wanted my two brothers to have some of the things they wanted. It was just that we could never ask for anything.

Before I finished high school, all my friends took the test to go to Taiwan for university. All my friends stayed at the library day and night, studying to pass the test. If your family was rich, you could put some money in the Korean University, and then they would let you get in. But the majority of everybody was not rich, so the majority of everyone went to Taiwan.

At the time I graduated high school, it seemed the whole of Korea—well, at least the Chinese people living in Korea—had gone to Japan to work. To work even for two, three months, even spending the airfare, would make them money. Obviously, they got a tourist visa to go there, so they were not supposed to be working, but they were, because the money was good.

My sister was already doing that at the time I finished high school. I told myself I just wanted to follow in her footsteps. If I did so, I knew I could make it. Initially, no one would lend me money for the airfare, which was rather expensive. Finally my uncle let me borrow the money, and I left Korea for the first time. I was only eighteen years old.

I couldn't go directly to Japan. Actually, I had to go to Taiwan first for the visa, so I went there first, and I stayed there for a couple of months.

Finding My Way In The World

Until the day I arrived in Taiwan, I had never eaten tropical fruit in my life. My sister bought a pineapple, and a bunch of bananas, and I ate the whole thing, twelve or more bananas and the entire pineapple, both very expensive fruits in Korea at that time. I ate the pineapple without the salt I now serve with it, and my whole mouth was swollen.

Besides the heavenly produce it brought forth, I didn't like the hot weather in Taiwan. The humidity really bothered me, but I stayed there for two months. Then I got a visa for Japan.

I went to Japan and joined my sister. We stayed with my aunt, who was already working there, in the little apartment she had. I worked in a coffee shop.

At the coffee shop, you made 80,000 yen, which is probably 800 US dollars today. At that time, it was worth a lot, because the exchange rate was different. Eight hundred dollars was big money, and I didn't spend anything.

I just took public baths.

The mama-san, which is what we called the woman owner of the coffee shop, really liked me, because I worked so hard, and with such detail. She liked me a lot. She gave me a bicycle to ride, and I finally got my own apartment, just one very small room, for a very cheap fifty or sixty dollars a month. You can't cook, or even do anything but sleep, in such a room, but it was my own.

In this little environment, everything was there that I needed.

From my apartment to the coffee shop, I could ride my bike to work. Every morning, for breakfast, they gave you a morning service, with one coffee, toast, and an egg. For lunch, you could have fried rice after the rush was over at 2:30, 3 o'clock in the afternoon, and then I could go home for a bath.

In the beginning, I was just working breakfast and lunchtime hours at the coffee shop. Later on, I joined my aunt at her evening job; my aunt, you see, was working at a club.

In Japan, men like to drink. Any time they drink, even when it's for work, with business partners, there must be a woman sitting next to them. They call their drinking establishments "clubs," perhaps to do justice to this extra service of having a hostess and to acknowledge the crucial business function drinking can have for their patrons.

The women who work in Japan's drinking clubs don't sleep with the men, but you do sit next to the men. You make sure the table is clean—they liked nice silverware. You have to put the lighter up to their cigarettes. If their drink runs out, you have to pour a new drink for them. It's not a high-class job, you know, and it's not a normal job.

And right now, I know there are a lot of young girls who are working at those places not because their family is poor; they want to buy more stuff for themselves. They want to buy name-brand things. That's why they work at those places.

But for us, we needed the money to send home. My aunt said, "Why do you work at the coffee shop? You only make 80,000 yen a month. You will make 10,000 yen a day at the club! That's over three times the money you're making at the coffee shop."

It tempted me a lot, perhaps because I was only eighteen years old. I was already making good money, but I decided I would work at the club. Soon after I started, I felt like I was already thirty years old.

In the beginning, it wouldn't bother me. My sister, my aunt, and I worked at the same place. We made good money, and we ate there, too, only for the nighttime meal as customers came in and ordered appetizers and things for the table. We ate, and practicing Japanese made us feel like we were learning, and they pay you well, too, so you don't feel bad anymore. If you work at those places long enough, however, you can get deeper and deeper in the hole.

I worked my first two-month period, and then extended my visa another two months, so I made good money. I didn't spend anything. I didn't. I only spent money on tickets, transportation, and taking public baths. That's all I spent, and the rest I saved. I didn't spend any money on eating. I didn't buy anything for myself. I saved all of my money and went home.

I gave it to my mom. Immediately, I wanted to go back to Japan, but I couldn't get in anymore. The visas kind of stopped. I could not get into Japan from Korea, and if I was to have any hope of getting in, I had to go back to Taiwan.

So I did. But even Taiwan was starting to get pretty serious. You could not get a visa, it seemed.

I had to stay in Taiwan for almost eight months, and eight months, I learned, is a long time, especially when you are not making money and you have to spend money buying something to eat, and stuff like that, every day. It hurts to spend even one penny when you can't make it back.

So for the first two months, I waited on the visa. I just thought it would come sooner, since they didn't give solid answers at the embassy. When I realized it wasn't coming, at the beginning of the third month, I found work there.

I worked at a T-shirt factory. They gave you a place to stay, and one meal to eat per day while you made 100 US dollars a month. I didn't have any skills, so what I did was pack T-shirts in clear plastic bags. I forget how many T-shirts I bagged, there were so many of them, but I stood at a big table sorting a massive pile of shirts into smaller shipments that would each fit one huge box.

I packed them into the clear bags. I put them in the box. I taped the box shut. That was my job, the job I did every single day. A lot of people made a little more money than me. They had a sewing skill, but I had none. Some ladies did the cutting, but I didn't have a desk, either, so all I did was packaging. But you know what? I was young, and I knew this was not a long-term job for me, nor would I work there for a long time if I could help it. "This job," I thought, "is to give me a place to eat, you know? They give me a place to sleep, you know?" This will help me for now. That's how I thought about things.

The things that I didn't like helped me think about different ways to make my time there better. I didn't like that the place was so dirty! And the mosquitoes were so bad! These things, and not knowing when I might be allowed to go back to Japan, made me think about other ways I could make money.

So finally, looking at the newspaper, I found a restaurant. This was a newer type of restaurant serving American-type of food: steak, hamburgers, fried shrimp. I said, "Wow, they just opened up, so they might be hiring!" I went there, and I said, "Uh, I don't have any skill, but I am a very hard-working person." The manager graduated from college, and his roommate was like me, Korean-born Chinese, and he said, "You guys work really hard...you're a hard-working people! I'm going to give you a chance." That was how I got the job.

The American-style restaurant also had a dorm. It wasn't exactly a nice dorm, but again, at least I could sleep and live there a little, and I could eat at the restaurant, where the work paid more than helping with the T-shirts at the factory, almost 300 US dollars a month, which made it a little better on the whole. And working as a waitress in Taiwan at the time, I was required to learn the Board of Health way to use a knife and keep the kitchen sanitary, and I did well at that, so I felt I was doing good.

A couple of months later, I was the manager. This coffee shop was owned by the manager's father-in-law, who was senior to him in a very wealthy family of Taiwanese. They felt they had to transfer their son over to the company of jewelers they also owned, so they needed a manager for the coffee shop, and he recommended me because I worked so hard. They gave me the job and a good raise.

Even after I made manager, although I was doing a good job, my heart was still in Japan, because I could make much more money for my family there. They paid me well, but there was no comparison, and I wanted nothing more than to go back. I was willing to stay in Taiwan and work as long as there was any chance I could get a visa for Japan, so I worked for about eight months, but when the visa suddenly came, I knew my chance had opened up, and I quit to go back to Japan.

The second time I went to Japan, I didn't go back to the same places I worked before. There were a lot of Korean clubs, and I liked a different place this time.

The new club had a head lady who knew my future husband, Robert "Rocky" Kang. Her husband was a good friend of his, and that's how I met Rocky.

I was nineteen the second time I went to work in Japan. Even at that age, you had to listen to the head lady. I believed you had to make them like you. Otherwise, I thought, they could give you a whole lot of trouble, so I was nice. I was young and nice and very much clinging to work as the centerpiece of my life. A lot of people I worked with didn't like it themselves, but I just cleaned. I didn't care, I just did that as a habit and a point of pride, and still do, so anywhere I go, people kind of like me, you know? This mama-san had just kind of been nice to me, and at that time my sister was not there anymore, so I felt very grateful for the kindness.

My sister had left Japan with her boyfriend. This left me alone, since my aunt had also returned to Korea when her latest two-month tourist visa expired. If you were lucky, you got one extension. If not, you had to go back and forth frequently.

I began going to this mama-san's house. My new club didn't give you a place to stay, which I would have welcomed as a chance to save more money, but I could still stick to my budget, and having a place to go and pass the time made it easier. That's why I followed this lady, went to her house, and, because she was so nice to me, I felt like cleaning mama-san's house while I was there.

Every time I went to mama-san's, Rocky was there.

They gambled a lot, big money. They liked to gamble; I liked to clean. They smoked a lot, so I dusted a lot, and every time I entered the room, Rocky was there. Then, later on, when she was being nice to me at work, she talked a lot about Rocky, and when I sensed that, I said, "Oh." I could see Rocky was not a bad person, which counted for a lot in the street life of which club hostesses were a part. I had kind of noticed that, at the edge of my awareness, for a while, and liked that about him. I suppose it's only natural that I began to like him, as a person.

After a time, when I went over to her house, it felt natural for Rocky to be there. Just like her husband and her, Rocky and I ate dinner together, time after time. They cleaned my dishes, graciously taking the task out of my hands when I tried to do it, and asked me to watch TV with Rocky, which helped teach me Japanese.

One night, I just slept over, even though Rocky was still there. We were just four people sleeping in one small room, the usual Japanese apartment. We did that for a long time, and, to me, it felt like we were meant to be together, this small family unit of Rocky, mama-san, her husband, and me as simple as it was to go around the room saying their names to myself without feeling uncomfortable: her, her husband, Rocky…me.

I slept there, and nothing happened. The next day I gathered my things to go back to my apartment, get ready, and go to work, but Rocky came to the door after me. He wanted to take me home in a cab. I said, "No, no, no, I don't want a ride. Cabs are too expensive. I can get around pretty good. I'll take a subway home, save money, you know?" That's why Rocky said I was different, for a young girl. He said, "You know exactly what you're doing," but he still—we still took a cab home, back to my apartment, you know? So that's how we got connected.

We've been together since that day. I found out he lived alone, without any family. He had no mother and no father. Although I did find out he had a brother, only one.

Rocky had a very tough life. They lived in a little Korean community in Osaka. He was born in Japan, the third generation of his family to live there. Still, even as a Japan-born Korean, he's more Korean than I am. I'm Chinese.

His grandma and grandpa went to Japan, and that's where his father was born, and then came Rocky and his brother.

They had a lot of money. I have a picture of him when he was three years old, and he had, like a crown on, you know?

And then, you know, at that time Japan was very poor, but their mom was very pretty. Really, really pretty. Because they were so wealthy, they had the money to hire a tutor to teach them English. At that time, you know, only rich people could do that. And from what I understand, this tutor was a Russian who spoke fluent English.

So they hired this person, and Rocky didn't tell me right at the beginning of our relationship, but later on, as we lived together for a long time, he told me: Rocky's mother ran away with the tutor. And later, she regretted it, and she wanted to come back, but you know what? At that time, the man had to worry about keeping up his face, and Rocky's father had a new face to protect since he had become the alderman of their little village, and so, though he was still in love with Rocky's mom, his father could not just let her come back. For the sake of his face, he didn't let her come back.

There is a beautiful lake, or lagoon, near their former home.

Rocky thinks there is a bridge or some kind of crossing there. Anyway, Rocky's mom went to this lagoon and drowned herself. I think Rocky was around three or four years old. I don't remember exactly the year.

Eventually, Rocky's father moved on and remarried. He married another Korean lady like Rocky's mother. He thought she would be a stepmother for his sons, and this woman was very nice to the brother, but she wasn't nice to Rocky, and later on this stepmother got a true daughter, so Rocky has a half-sister.

Still Rocky's father couldn't get over his first wife, so he began gambling a lot. He gambled everything away—even his house.

And later on, when Rocky was fourteen or fifteen years old, his father committed suicide in the same place as his mom, in the same lake. After his father's death, the stepmother took the daughter and just moved away, leaving Rocky and his brother.

Rocky's brother was very smart, okay? Very, very smart, but although he was smart, he was also in and out of jail a lot. So he never did take care of Rocky. Rocky was sort of like surviving by himself: going to this house, going to that house, you know? Eventually, this one family kind of took care of him a lot. This family was a Mafia family.

The son was a Mafia. Not the head boss, but he was a pretty, pretty high boss there. So he, and they, kind of took care of Rocky a lot, and Rocky had nowhere to go, so he went there.

Then Rocky started working in the coffee shop—they had a coffee shop on the first floor. Rocky worked at the coffee shop, and then Rocky dated this Mafioso's sister.

Rocky just naturally took to this family. They were part of his family...they were his second family, you know?

One time, he went to Korea to visit with, like, a group. When he came back, he found out his girlfriend—the boss's sister—had fooled around with somebody else.

Rocky found that out because one of Rocky's friends told

him. They had already been talking about marriage. In fact, they had already tried to set the date, and the others, especially the girl's father, already thought that the marriage was going to go on. When they found out about her infidelity, they came to apologize to Rocky, but Rocky didn't take it well. Right after he finished with the sister, I came in.

In Japan, the Mafia are called "Yakuza." Yakuza have, like, a special way of talking so that people kind of get scared. They have their own Mafia language.

No matter where I saw him. Everywhere I saw him, he didn't look like a Yakuza. Some Yakuza sell drugs. If not drugs, they do gambling. You can bet on football, baseball, everything. Some do the killing, you know? Yakuzas have boss, boss, boss, boss.

Rocky made his money from gambling. He gambled, and he took people's money for bets, and that's how he made money, making the telephone calls to place the bets. When people call in bets, they go through him, and he's mean, to make sure the people pay for their gambling debts. If you don't pay, then he talks like a Yakuza, and people get scared. Then he sends the other people after you. They threaten you, so people get scared.

I found out all of this later, but in the beginning, when I first met Rocky, I didn't know. This lady, the head lady, told me, "Oh no!" When I specifically asked her, "Is Rocky a Yakuza?" Because only Yakuza could spend big money coming to the club. People cannot spend that kind of money coming in, only Yakuza, and Rocky came to the club and spent lots of money.

He came to the club with this lady's husband... I don't know if they were married. Whatever. This man came with Rocky, and when they came in, one time he would spend and one time Rocky. When they came in, I would go sit with them. She would sit there, too, and then this other lady, too.

I was eager to learn Japanese, you know? So, there was one TV program that came on about 3:30 in the afternoon, the time

I was home after taking a public bath. I would come home and get ready to go to my night work, and I always watched it: it was a show about Yakuza. I liked the story. I needed to see my Yakuza program. I got so scared, you know? It was like, "If you don't listen, they threaten you! And some bad Yakuza, they even tell you to go on the street—they sell you into prostitution, and then they come and take all your money away! You have to support them!" Some are worse, some are…you know?

So I asked her specifically. "Rocky is not a Yakuza, is he? Is Rocky a Yakuza?" Looking at the outside, you really cannot tell.

"No, no, no, no, he works for an office."

And I was so naive, you know, that I believed her. I really believed her when she said that.

I lived in a neighborhood that was not a good area. A lot of gangsters lived there, a lot of Mafia, which made it pretty dangerous, especially at nighttime. One night I had a guy follow me from the train station all the way to my apartment. I got so scared. I felt it would be even more dangerous to try to get into the safety of my apartment with him on my heels. My sister and my aunt had already warned me to run from these urban stalkers—if I ever noticed a man following me before I reached my stop, I was supposed to get off the train and run away. But this guy was following me in my neighborhood. I walked around and around, in a panic, until I lost him. It was very late when I finally got into my apartment, and I was terrified. Since then, I had been living in fear. So when Rocky offered me the chance to go and live with him at his apartment, I said yes right away.

We had already slept together at the time. He lived downtown, so I could walk to work without having to take a train or anything, and he lived alone, and he was nice. He was really nice to me. Now that I put it in words, that's the whole reason we got together, okay?

And, you know, when he helped me move to his apartment, I

thought it was so funny that he didn't take his shirt off. Even when we slept together, he didn't take his shirt off. The first time, and the second time, it didn't catch up to me, but then, I started to think: "Why is his shirt always on?"

He always had just, like, a polo shirt, and he always kept that on, you know? I was like, "you know?" Question marks started coming in. So finally, one day when I was getting to know him more and more, and we could joke a little more, I opened Rocky's shirt.

I didn't speak a lot of Japanese at that time, you know? I had only been there for a total time of not even eight months, so I didn't speak a lot of Japanese. With a very, like, crude vocabulary, like "boom, boom, boom," I could get by.

I was shocked to find tattoos all over his back. All over, all the way up to his neck, you know, everywhere. In Japan, only the Yakuza put on tattoos.

The next thing I started begging Rocky not to hurt me. Using the most polite Japanese I could, I pleaded: "Rocky, please don't harm me, okay? Please don't harm me! I have a mother and father to support. I have two brothers. I have to make money to support them. Please don't hurt me."

He didn't say anything. The next day, I went back to the sister.

"Didn't you tell me he's not a Yakuza? He has the tattoos!" I was so mad.

"Oh, no, Keiko," she said. I was using the name "Keiko" as my Japanese name in the bar, in the club, you know? "Keiko, those tattoos come from when he was young. He played...he, he fooled around for a little bit. He put it on, but he's really not a Yakuza. Look at how nice he is."

Rocky was really nice, really, really nice, so I believed what I wanted. I didn't want to believe Rocky was a Yakuza. Yeah, and from then on, whatever he said, I believed what I could. I refused to believe that the first man who had ever been nice to me was not a good person. My mind just would not let me believe that because Rocky did many small things to make me happy.

In the middle of work, Rocky would call me down, you know? One time he brought a big teddy bear for me. And he would take me out to eat. He knew I liked seafood. He knew I didn't eat meat. I was not a vegetarian, but I was just not crazy about meat. He would take me to the crab house and buy a huge, big crab for me, which was very expensive. Crab was very expensive. I finished everything by myself. I didn't even offer him any. I didn't say, "Would you like some?" In my life, I had never eaten something like that before. He took me out for dinner almost every other day, you know? It was a really good time, a really, really good time. He was really nice to me, so I believed her the day she said, "Look at how nice he is to you."

And I didn't see him talk like the Yakuza or anything. The only thing I noticed was that he didn't seem to be working or anything. That kind of made me suspicious. She said, "Oh, he's working at night. With my husband."

"Okay, then I believe it," I said.

I continued to live on my beliefs for as long as I could. One day I was cleaning up for him at the apartment and found a little finger. It was an imitation finger, like a fake finger, just one part of one finger. I knew that in the Japanese Yakuza, if you did something bad, you could take a finger out, cut it out and take it to your boss as a sacrifice. Then, if you mess up again, they cut you again and give that part of a finger to the boss again. You know, to ask for forgiveness.

I was like, "Oh, my God, why is this here?" So that night, when he was sleeping, I opened his hand up. One of Rocky's fingers had been cut off, but I didn't know that. Then I could not longer deny that he was part of the Yakuza.

The next day, when Rocky woke up, I could not hold my anger.

"Rocky, I found out you have no finger. I'm very scared, because I was watching that Yakuza program on television, and if anything happens to me...I have to support my family, okay? Rocky, please don't harm me."

By that time though, I knew Rocky was a nice person. Maybe he was missing a finger, and he had tattoos, but overall he was a really nice person, really, really nice. I decided that I liked him as a person. I didn't like that he was a Yakuza, but I could not change that and neither could he. When you join the Yakuza that is a choice for life. They do not let you leave the Yakuza.

After that, I started to learn more about Rocky's Yakuza friends. He started taking me to see them. He took me to his boss's place. He had to take me because I was living with him, I was part of his life, and his boss had the right to know everything about him.

More than just taking me to see his boss, Rocky had to introduce me. I was very scared. I couldn't even see straight, I was so scared of the boss, but his wife was really, really nice. And it seemed like everybody looked at me a little differently, because Rocky had just finished the relationship with the boss's sister, and I didn't know that. I didn't know anything about that until we came to America.

My visa came to an end, and so I had to go back to Korea. While I was home, Rocky was calling me up.

"All day I think about you," he would say. You could tell he really missed me, and so I applied for a visa to go back. That time, I got a visa right away, and I went back to Japan within two weeks.

I was really, really sick with a bad flu complete with a fever and everything, but as soon as I got back, I went back to work. All while I was sick, Rocky was taking care of me really good. Usually Asian men don't care, you know? But he was really taking care. I kind of felt the warmth, because I didn't have any male who was nice to me growing up. My father was never there to be nice to me, you know, so I didn't know what that felt like. Rocky was probably the first person that was really nice to me, okay?

I had come back to Japan for Rocky, but I really did not have a plan for the future. Then one day, my sister sent me an application to Roosevelt University in Chicago, Illinois. My sister didn't know anything about Rocky…zero. All she knew was that I should not be staying in Japan, working in those kinds of places, for a long time. You kind of get into the same water, the underworld, that Rocky had gotten involved in. My sister was living in Chicago with my older brother and her boyfriend.

She wanted to bring me to America to be with her, but she didn't know anything about Rocky, so when I got the application, I cried. Oh, I cried. I cried, and Rocky didn't know what I was crying for. Later, I told him.

"I want to go to America. I don't want to live in Japan. I don't want to stay here. They call me names. I don't want to work here, because you have to laugh with them. You know what it's like… You're selling yourself. You're selling your personality to please other people. I don't like to work in those places, and you are a Yakuza. We don't have a good future, okay? I don't want to live in Japan. I want to go to America. But I don't want to leave you behind. I know you're not going to come with me…"

Because he was a Yakuza, he wasn't going to come with me. He couldn't come with me.

I was crying, crying, crying. Really, I was crying for, like, three days: day and night. Finally, Rocky said, "You know, give me a week to think about it." I was like, "Oh, just to think about it!" I was like, "Oh my God, something could be happening!"

We were really nice together. He was really nice to me, and I was really nice to him, too.

I think he didn't wait for a week to go by. Three days later, he said, "Let's go. But we're not going to take anything, okay? We cannot let people notice we are going to go someplace."

We left everything the way it was. We left just like we were going to a restaurant to eat, okay? So we just left everything behind. I brought nothing with me. Maybe we took an extra pair of underwear, and we left.

Living The American Dream

We went to Korea first, to see my mom and dad. That was the first time Rocky saw my two brothers, too, and from Korea, we flew direct to Los Angeles.

I didn't know you were supposed to book your tickets all the way to your final destination, so we didn't have tickets to carry us through to Chicago when we arrived in Los Angeles. We had to fly first class, on the red eye.

I had, like, about $5,000 or $6,000: the money from my work in Japan. I took the money with me to Korea, and then to the United States, and that was all the money I had. The tickets cost $500 each. When they asked me for $500, we knew it was expensive, but we didn't have anywhere else to go, so we just paid it. $1,000, okay?!

Rocky didn't have any money. He gambled all of his money away when we were living in Japan, so he didn't leave with any savings. Any time he had money, he spent it. He's not like me. I'm the saver.

Of course, back in Japan, I hadn't minded when Rocky spent a little money on me. Rocky and I met in the springtime, maybe in May, because June is my birthday, and I remember that right after we met, he gave me a jewelry box that was my first birthday gift for all my life.

Until that time, you know, I never had a birthday gift. Nobody ever had a cake for me. Nobody ever sent me anything. My parents never did anything. For our birthdays, we just ate noodles. Noodles are long, so if we ate them, we would have a long life. Rocky was the first person to give me a present, and I still have that jewelry box at home.

On the plane, they asked, "Would you like to have a sandwich?" I had trouble understanding what they were asking. Of course, I couldn't understand a word of English. Then we came to Chicago. My sister knew I was coming, but she didn't know the date I would arrive. So when I tried to use the payphone to call her, I didn't know how. I didn't know which coin to put in. I tried to ask this guy, but he was kind of rushed. "Oh," he said, "just put this in." I put one quarter in, but it wouldn't work, so we were standing there at O'Hare Airport like two stupid people.

Finally, I saw a Chinese man passing by, and I said to him, "Please, please, I need to dial this number!" He explained to me in Chinese that to dial Lake Forest from O'Hare Airport, I had to put in more than one quarter. He dialed for me, and my sister answered. It was early morning, 6 or 7 o'clock, so my sister and her boyfriend came to the airport.

The minute they came to the airport, they were shocked. I was not alone. My oldest brother was really shocked when he found out about Rocky, too, because he was also expecting his sister to be alone, and his sister came with her...boyfriend. Rocky was my boyfriend, yes, and my brother was expecting me to come alone.

They were shocked, for a little while, but you know, we drove to Denny's and had breakfast, and after that, they took us home. We spent that day resting. We didn't do anything.

My brother and sister were living in a two-bedroom, single-family house, with two bedrooms and a den. My sister and her boyfriend slept in one bedroom, and my brother gave Rocky and me his room. Later on, my sister and her boyfriend moved to the basement. Rocky and I and my brother used the two bedrooms.

The day after we arrived, I tried to do the laundry. I was used to hand washing, you know? So I went downstairs in the basement, where they had this two-compartment laundry sink. I didn't know how to use washing machines. While I was down there, I felt like somebody was watching me. I turned my head up, and there was a snake! A huge, huge, big snake was looking at me, right outside the glass of the window. I don't know how I ran upstairs. I mean...I woke up everyone. My sister's boyfriend grabbed the broom.

When they came down to the basement, the snake was gone, but they saw the snake's huge, big hole outside, so they put dirt down there. I didn't like to see the snake at all, and even though they filled the hole with dirt, I couldn't go down to the basement after that day. I was just too scared.

On our second day in Chicago, Rocky started as the dishwasher in my brother's restaurant. I had a few more days off, and then I started as a bus girl. Rocky had no machine to help him. He had to wash all the dishes by hand, and Rocky had beautiful hands, because he had never worked with his hands, you know? He had prettier hands than I have. I don't have good hands, because I work so hard with them all my life.

Rocky had very nice hands, but he started to wash dishes. On the weekend, there could be twenty buckets lined up there, which we had to sort when I finished my job, my bus girl job.

I was a bus girl, working alongside another bus boy, and my sister and her boyfriend were waiter and waitress. Rocky and my brother were the people in the kitchen. Business was good, and, working as a bus girl, I received a little bit of my sister's tips. My brother gave Rocky and me each $500 a month, so we made $1,000 a month and took one day off. We didn't pay rent, so once in a while we went shopping at Sunset Foods, where we would spend $20 or $30 to buy a whole bunch of stuff.

My sister started to teach me English and teach Rocky and me how to drive. I learned how to ask, "Now, what would you like to drink?" I started to memorize the names of all of the liquors. "Vodka tonic, blah, blah, blah." I learned the wine—"Chablis?"

Next I learned the names of foods: "Want to buy a crab?" I started to memorize all of those things when I was a bus girl.

Then, later on, after I learned the menu items, my sister let me take one table at a time, so I did well. "I do one table good." Then she let me take another table, and later on, she let me be in charge of a little bit of the restaurant.

Those were rich people, you know, in Lake Forest, Illinois. This gentleman came in—I think there were two people sitting at the table, and I think this old gentleman was asking for sweet-and-sour sauce, but I gave him soy sauce. For me, it was not easy to tell the difference between sweet-and-sour and soy sauce, and when I looked at the different kinds of people in America, I couldn't tell the difference between all the white and black people I was meeting. Many things seemed the same to me.

I think, one way or the other, he asked for one sauce and I brought another. He gave me a very nasty look. The body language gave me a very odd feeling, okay? So I went to the bathroom, and I cried. I felt so ashamed, I was crying.

My sister followed me a short while later and asked, "What happened?"

"I took the wrong sauce!"

"You feel stupid for that, and you're crying? You can't survive in America," she said.

Rocky was still doing the dishwashing, and when there were no dishes to wash, he would peel the shrimp, wash the vegetables, and do whatever else a kitchen helper can do.

Even later on, I started to not just give the customers what they wanted, but have little conversations with them. People seemed to be very nice.

And we started to go to school. We went to the College of Lake County in Waukegan, Illinois. It was not the main campus of the College, just a small school, with just one office, but it was free. You can go there and take English, as an immigrant, and later I got a driver's license there. The easy classes were on Monday and Wednesday, and Tuesdays and Thursdays were a little harder, a little higher level. I knew a little bit more than Rocky. He went to the easy classes on Monday and Wednesday. I went to the easy and the difficult classes for six months, Monday, Tuesday, Wednesday, Thursday, so I learned a lot.

The course didn't just teach English. It taught us how to read the newspaper and a lot of basic things that you need to know in America, like "When you drive, you have to have insurance, blah, blah, blah, blah," just the education you have to have to live like a normal person in America.

It was so funny sometimes. When we got a car, the first place we went was McDonald's. I fell in love with the fish filet sandwich. I can eat three or four of them, you know? I would say, "Fish sandwich," and they wouldn't understand. They kept on repeating, "Filet." I said, "Fish," they kept repeating "Filet." I didn't know a "filet" is a fish sandwich, okay? The lady got frustrated so she decided she wouldn't take care of me, and I was left out as she started to take care of someone behind me. Then, later on, I realized, "Oh, 'filet of fish' and 'fish sandwich' are the same thing! Okay!" For us, driving to McDonald's to buy a fish sandwich was a huge, big thing, especially when I was able to drive there in my own car.

Yeah, we bought a car! A brand-new car, with all the money I brought from Asia. We didn't have credit, so I paid everything down for a Chevy Camaro. We had a car to drive to McDonald's, and we were working steadily, so I was happy.

Having a car made a huge difference for us. It made it easier to go to school and work. We also took our first trip into the city of Chicago. We went shopping, and I bought one skirt. It cost $30. My God was that expensive. Then Rocky wanted to see a movie. Not knowing where to find the movie theaters, we drove around and around for four hours! Rocky wanted to see an x-rated movie, called *Deep Throat*. Every time we tried to find the theater we ended up on Milwaukee Avenue. Ten times we ended up on Milwaukee Avenue! After four hours, we found the movie theater by accident.

Rocky started to help out in the kitchen, in addition to washing dishes. If there weren't a lot of dishes, he washed and cut vegetables or peeled the shrimp.

We waitresses had to do everything. Our brother never took care of his place. It was more like my sister and me and Rocky and my brother-in-law.

My brother was a brilliant restaurateur, yet impulsive. He hadn't exactly needed to save money to start the restaurant. As he had done in Korea, he just built it himself. Well, in this case, he rented the space, and did the interior himself. If you could have seen inside, you would have been amazed. He used cheap bamboo, but it looked so beautiful. He is a very creative, very smart person.

The customers were nice, very high-class people, because it was a pretty famous restaurant in Lake Forest, Illinois, at the time.

It was called North China.

Movie stars would go there. My brother got a lot of movie star pictures for his walls because a movie was shot in Lake Forest, and the stars ate at the restaurant all the time.

He just had a natural knack for cooking. He was a very creative cook, too.

When he first came to America, he stayed in Los Angeles, working in a Korean restaurant, but of course his youthful experience of starting his own restaurant had already proven he had the talents needed to go into business.

He had the natural talent to put the seasons together in his dishes, so each of his dishes was just very good. He was talented in cooking timing-wise, an important area of Chinese cooking. Using the wok wisely keeps the colors naturally beautiful.

Now I will describe the inside of the restaurant. It was wonderful. The interior was, like, an off white and green, a beautiful combination. He had green curtains and carpets and bamboo-and-rattan chairs. There was a little water fountain on the wall that looked perfect.

North China seated about seventy people, which made it a medium-size restaurant, as is confirmed by the fact that they had a hard liquor license.

When Rocky and I both worked there, we each got $500 to work six days a week. We didn't put our cash in the bank, we just brought it home and pooled it together, but I was our banker. Whenever he got money, he just gave it to me. I put it right into our home-based savings.

And he never had more than $5 in his wallet. I was very strict on how we spent our money. Our only entertainment was when we went out for hot dogs and a movie each week. The hot dogs cost $2 and the movie cost $1.50. Once Rocky spent $3, and I got very angry with him. I yelled at him for such a long time. That is why he never had more than $5, so we could always save money.

My sister always showed me around. After she and her boyfriend bought a house in Lake Bluff, she took me to see a model house, and I fell in love. I fell in love with those model houses. I said, "Oh God, in my dreams, can I live in this kind of house, with a baby's room, and a kids' room?" That's when I started dreaming of the American dream.

Exactly one year later, we bought a condo. We took all the money we had and paid a down payment that was still $3,000 short, if I remember correctly, but we borrowed money from both my sister and my brother. It was a two-bedroom condo on the first floor.

We were just so happy, and we didn't have any furniture, or anything, really. We had one queen mattress bed, so we put it on the top of our car and moved in.

The night we moved in, I had a pot to cook noodles in, but after I cooked them, I realized I didn't have a bowl, or chopsticks to eat with. The availability of chopsticks wasn't like it is now, when you can get chopsticks at so many stores and plastic cutlery is everywhere. Nowadays we could have gone to McDonald's and grabbed some plastic forks. I didn't have access to anything like that on five minutes' notice, nor did I even have a table and chairs. So what did we do? We put newspaper on the kitchen floor and had a picnic in our own house. We were so hungry from the labor of moving that we just kind of figured out how we were going to share from the pot and started eating. We drank the soup first, and used our fingers to finish the noodles. That was the most memorable meal of my life.

I felt very close to Rocky then, there was no doubt about it. I knew we were close. We worked together, we went home together, we did everything together, and we only had each other.

But I always felt I had to do more from the beginning when we came to America. I felt Rocky sacrificed himself to come to America. He didn't have to come to America and work. He came because I was crying, so I felt like he came, you know, because of me. From the beginning, I said to myself, "I have to work harder to make our dream come true, you know?" I had heavier shoulders than his. I felt sorry for asking him to sacrifice himself, and that I have to work harder, harder, harder, okay?

After we bought a condo, life was pretty normal. Every day we went to work, you know, and we didn't have furniture or anything inside the house. That's when I fell in love with garage sales. A wonderful Japanese neighbor told me about a garage sale. I also find them myself, too. You see the garage sale sign, go and look at the things. So almost everything in our house, I bought from the garage sale.

I still have one chair; I have the chair in my house. It isn't reupholstered, but still, I just love it the way it is. It's the only brand new thing I bought. All the rest is garage sale, garage sale, garage sale, garage sale. But I was so happy. I learned to look through the newspaper every Thursday and Friday morning for sales, you know? My brother's restaurant didn't open for lunch, so we didn't get to work until 2 o'clock in the afternoon. So in the morning, I would find the garage sales. I bought everything there. But I didn't just buy things for myself; I even bought things for my sister. Before we bought a condo, my sister, they bought a house, a very small house. So I would buy things at the garage sales for her, too.

Although we, eventually, all moved out from my brother's house, for a time we stayed at his restaurant. But that changed, too. I can't remember if it was my sister who left the place first. My sister and her husband both said they couldn't handle my older brother's frequent absence from the restaurant.

They left to work for somebody else, and I couldn't stay with my brother, either, because he truly WASN'T ever there. It was so hard, and finally I left the restaurant, too.

I went to work for a Japanese steak house. At that time, my English was still not very good, but it was good enough to take the orders, and I spoke Korean, and Japanese, which was perfect for the Japanese steak house, because the people there had hired a majority of Korean waitresses in between the few Japanese waitresses, making it easy for me to communicate, speaking all those languages.

As I was starting to work there, Rocky still worked at my brother's. At that time, Rocky was becoming a cook, moving there from his position as a food preparer. When my brother was in a good mood, he would teach Rocky to cook. If not, no, but that is how Rocky stayed there after we had all left.

Later on, the restaurant just gradually closed down, because my brother was never there, and Rocky was not able to take care of the restaurant.

And then, because they closed down, he said, the authorities forced them to give up their liquor license. He might have had some violations, I don't know every little detail, but the restaurant just closed down.

After that Rocky came to work at the steak house, too. Then he had to go back to Japan to take care of some kind of paperwork. This kind of paperwork takes about a good six months to take care of, and you have to wait there.

Rocky wasn't afraid of the Yakuza punishing him for leaving by the time he went back to Japan. By that time, they pretty much already knew he came from a higher class, now, so they accepted it.

And Rocky himself was happy he came with me, I'm sure of it. He did well working hard in America. Also, Rocky's brother was still in Japan, so that's who he stayed with, so he was doubly okay.

His brother found out where Rocky was two months after we came to America but, of course, did not tell the Yakuza. Eventually, Rocky's friend told his brother he went to America, so he kind of knew his brother was okay, and then he had it confirmed when they saw each other again. He sort of watched Rocky grow up in the hard life, and without their parents, so I guess, somehow, he was happy, on the inside, that he came with me. He didn't really want Rocky to live that hard life.

When I was taking him to leave, I was pretty sad. I was crying, because we would have to separate for six months.

Rocky was so nice, I think, to look for a job while he was back in Japan that time, because we didn't have a lot of money but what I myself was making to pay the mortgage.

I stayed here, working, and went from one restaurant to another, and I found out you learn a lot when you do this. At every restaurant, there's a good part to learn. Every restaurant has a negative side, too. I saw a lot, so I said, "Oh, this restaurant is really good on this. Oh, this restaurant is not good at that." I was kind of like picking things up fast. And at every restaurant I went to, I worked very hard.

I didn't take birth control pills with Rocky for all those years, but I never got pregnant. Well, okay, I did get pregnant in Japan when I first met him. And yes, I had an abortion. After that, I didn't get pregnant at all. I didn't protect against pregnancy in any way.

Rocky was in Japan for exactly six months. When he came back, I got pregnant right away, and I didn't even know.

I went to my sister's house, and I was cutting the grass and my stomach hurt me so much that I stopped and almost immediately went to check with my doctor's office. They said I had been pregnant for two months.

I worked until my seventh month of pregnancy.

Rocky went back to the steakhouse after he got back from Japan. He went there to work as a sushi chef at a cook's pay, and he worked lunch and dinner. When he came home, he went to bed right away. When he got up, he went to work immediately, so I didn't see him all day. I would think about it sometimes: "I'm always left by myself. When I go out, I see other couples. Wife pregnant, husbands walking them around the little pond in the park near our condo. It just looks so beautiful, but when Rocky comes home, I don't have that." I really didn't have that. He came home; he went to bed; he woke up; he went to work.

On his day off, he just wanted to sleep. But I kind of wanted him to go for those walks with me, so we could talk, like those other couples.

We didn't make special plans to walk and talk before I got pregnant, but at least we had had something in common, which was working together and then coming home together. We had something. After he started working at the steak house for lunch and dinner, we didn't have a lot of things to talk about.

Finally, in the eighth month of pregnancy, I got so angry. "I think he's sleeping a little too much." I said, "If you want to sleep this much, why don't you go back to Japan?"

I got so angry that day. I just packed his clothes in a bag.

In the process of writing this book, my publisher asked me, quite directly, "Was Rocky happy you were pregnant?"

I didn't see the big emotions with Rocky, ever. That's what I call the "Asian man syndrome."

But I can remember how he reacted when I first got pregnant in Japan. He was sad—it was sad, the whole situation, because we felt we could not keep the baby. I was too young, and together we just were not stable.

For one thing, I didn't want to live in Japan. And how well did we know each other? I got pregnant less than six months after we met. We met in May, and I know I got pregnant in the wintertime.

Abortions are very, very common in Japan and Korea, I think. Rocky came to the clinic with me because I didn't speak a lot of Japanese.

After I had the abortion, I was so cold. I went to Rocky's boss's house. The boss's wife made a very hot noodle dish for me. I remember them as the most delicious noodles I had ever had. After those noodles I felt so, so good.

But not when I was carrying Mari. Rocky left for Japan when I was eight months pregnant. I didn't even know he had gone at first. After we fought about his sleeping that night, he got up in the morning, took the bag—I had packed—took the car, and went to the airport.

I thought he went to work, until the restaurant called to ask where he was, letting me know he hadn't come to work. I still didn't imagine that he had left, but it was then that I realized this thing was getting pretty serious.

I started to cry, and cry, and cry. "I don't know what to do. I don't have a car. I don't even have work to go to, to have the option of going to work."

Finally, my brother's girlfriend at the time, now my sister-in-law, took me out to look for the car. Well, we found it at the airport, which is when we realized he had left.

I brought the car home and called Japan.

I got Rocky on the phone, and he said, "Yes, I am in Japan, and I won't come back..."

Finally, the restaurant's Japanese chef, who turned out to live in a condo across the street from ours, although we hadn't realized it at the time, made a call to Rocky and convinced him to come back to me.

I had borrowed $5,000 to have the baby, to pay for the delivery and such, and suddenly I had to send Rocky $3,000 to buy a ticket and come back here.

I laugh now to remember how I thought, "So that's my deliver-baby-money gone."

One month later, he came back. Everything went back to normal again, although normal meant dissatisfaction for me.

He went back to work, and I waited for the baby to come.

And it was still the same thing. He slept a lot, and he was never there for me.

Before the baby was born, we did talk about the delivery day. He told me if it was a girl, he was going to throw it in the garbage, because Asian people are pretty much into the boys, you know? It was a shock to hear Rocky say that, but I could understand, too, because the typical Asian man is like that. I just thought, "Hopefully, it's a boy."

On December 23rd, around midnight, my stomach started getting pains. I remember I was mopping the floor, even that late at night, because I just didn't want to go to sleep, so I started to clean the house and mop the kitchen...

I told Rocky, "I think I have to go to the hospital," and I couldn't believe what he said. "Do you have to deliver the baby now? Can't I sleep a little more?"

Finally, we went to the hospital. After eighteen hours, the baby wouldn't come, so the doctor had to give me a caesarean section. The minute the doctor told me, my tears come out.

"It's not that you have to cut my stomach," I explained. "I don't have money." I tried to make him understand.

"I don't even have money for any more delivery. How much will the c-section cost?"

"$10,000," he said.

At that time, Rocky and I didn't know there was such a thing as Public Aid. We thought we would have to pay for it right away ourselves.

But you do have to actually deliver the baby while you're at it, and I had gone through so much pain after eighteen hours. I agreed to the surgery. Even afterward, my stomach hurt so much that I had to ask the nurses why they still hadn't delivered my baby. One of them said, "Oh, no, you had a baby girl, congratulations!"

Mari's face was like a Xerox copy of Rocky's. My stomach was cut, so I couldn't laugh without it hurting a lot, but I started to laugh, they were so identical.

After one day at the hospital, I told the doctor I wanted to check out.

"I don't have the money to stay here."

"No, you have to stay here for three or four days," he said.

"If I stay more, YOU have to pay for me!" So after two days, he let me go.

The weather was really cold the day we took Mari home. My mom came over and helped me. I couldn't go to work, so Rocky worked alone. My mother helped me cook, and kept me company, since Rocky was still the same: go to work; come home; go to work; come home. He was never a person who wanted to take care of the baby. If she cried in the middle of the night, it was always me who had to pick her up, not the father. All he was was the man who had fathered her. He wasn't doing anything, really not a thing.

When Mari was one month old, I had to go back out to work, because we owed the hospital money and had to pay them back. The formulas were already getting very expensive, so I wanted to breast-feed Mari, but it wouldn't come out in the beginning. Finally, after the first month, milk began to flow just in time for me to go back to work.

At the time, there was a Chinese restaurant opening up, so I went there to ask for a waitress job. The only potential problem was I had gained a lot of weight in pregnancy, so their uniform wouldn't fit me, so I put on a wonderful Chinese coat I had and worked for them as a waitress.

I wanted to breast-feed Mari, not because of its rumored health benefits and effectiveness in bonding mother and child, but simply because formula seemed so expensive to me. I wanted to breast feed because if I can save one dollar, I will.

When I went out to work, it was so hard to have chosen a restaurant, because I had to work for lunch and dinner, so I fed Mari, in the morning, before I took her to be watched by my mom at my sister's house.

My mother was willing to take care of Mari, but I said, "I will give you $200 a month." So, as she has with every child born to my sister, my brothers and me, my mom took care of Mari.

After the lunch rush at work, I went back to my mom at my sister's house to breast-feed Mari again. I had about two hours' time before I had to go back to work.

Weeknights weren't so bad. You finish early, and I didn't have to eat dinner there, so I could go home early, but the problem was on the weekends. If you take good care of late customers, which you have to do, you can't leave until very late. Even then, I wouldn't have minded taking care of more tables, but when the time came, my breasts wanted the baby.

One Saturday night, I was taking care of the orders of four people who had come in quite close to closing time. Milk started dripping from my breasts onto my clothing. I needed to take care of my body, as I felt the warmth of the milk coming out. I thought, "Oh my gosh, oh my God, Mari is home hungry, and here my breasts are coming, I can feel it, and I have to take care of this table!" Finally, after I took the order and put it in the kitchen, I went to get the breast pump I had left in the bathroom in a cabinet under the sink. I had to pump all the breast milk I could then put away the bottle for safekeeping. My breasts were so wet when I finished pumping that I had to put some hand towels inside my bra so that more would not leak onto my clothing when I went back to finish the table. Still it was not enough, and by the end of the night, my uniform was soaked with milk.

When I went home on those nights, I stopped to pick up Mari then went to my house.

That was the most difficult time I remember, those months of work to repay the ten thousand dollar loan to the hospital. We paid it all back within one year. So much for Public Aid!

I was really having fun at the restaurant, though. The manager at the time became a close friend, Ling, who I've now known for a very long time.

Soon after Mari was born, my brother-in-law opened a restaurant in Chicago, and he needed a waitress. Their restaurant was in Lincoln Park, right next to the famous Park West Theater. I was the perfect person to be their waitress, and I thought it would be pretty good for me because I could just go to work and come back home in one car with my brother-in-law.

All I had to do was drive to their house at the beginning of our workday, which was not in the morning, because we didn't have to be at work until lunchtime, and leave Mari with my mom.

Rocky and I did the same routine for a long time. Rocky woke up in the morning and went to his steak house, and I woke up a little bit later, took care of Mari, then brought her to my mother at my sister's house and went to work with my brother-in-law. We worked all day long, and when I came home, Rocky would have come in before me and was already asleep.

Finally, my sister decided to move to the city. I thought we should move there, too, and then my brother opened up a sushi place as the follow-up to his Chinese restaurant, and Rocky wanted to work for him there. If we were both working in the city, I thought we had no reason to live so far north of Chicago in Vernon Hills, Illinois.

So what we did was rent out the condominium to cover the mortgage, and then we rented an apartment to stay in on Sheridan, over by Hollywood, on the North Side of Chicago. It was a very bad apartment, with cockroaches and mice running around every night, and the neighborhood was full of stolen cars and police sirens, but it only cost $230. Still, the only reason we ended up in a place that bad was that I trusted a Korean friend who was married to a man from Rocky's old job at the steak house, who lived in that building, who kept encouraging us to move there, saying "Okay, it's a little nasty around here, but it's okay living here, and it's so cheap, $230!" She said it so often, that's why I can still remember the exact rent we paid. It turned out the landlord gave her and her husband $50 for quieting my fears and reeling us in.

So yes, we lived there, but I quit the job at my brother-in-law's place, and I couldn't find a new job, so I didn't work. We still had Rocky's income from the sushi place, but we needed more than one income.

My mom came and stayed with Mari while I looked for a job that I could hold down with only one car between Rocky and me.

Then I got sucked into watching videotapes of this Korean soap opera. You rent like ten or twelve of them, and I had nothing to do, so I could finish them in one night, if I stayed up all night. When I was watching soap operas in this hardcore way, I didn't care if Rocky came home or anything. I just wanted to watch one after another after another, and I knew this wasn't good, but I learned it from my friend. It felt like something had happened to me, but I still wanted to work in a Chinese or Japanese restaurant.

So finally I called a very high-toned, classy Japanese restaurant called Shino. They asked me to come in for an interview, so Rocky, on his day off, and Mari got in the car with me to go to the interview, and they said they wanted to hire me, so that was good.

My friend wasn't working, so I asked her to take care of Mari for me when I went back to work. I gave her a little money.

This Japanese restaurant, which is not there any longer, incidentally, was not big, but very classy, so in the beginning the mama-san wouldn't allow me to take care of the Japanese customers. Later on she found out I really worked hard and did a good job, so not long after I started she began sending me all the way to the front of the house to take care of the customers. They only had the top Japanese people coming, you know, the people from Tokyo Bank and Mitsubishi; all of those high, high-end Japanese company people went there.

At the same time, Rocky had a co-worker at the sushi restaurant who said, "Oh, I was passing by Sheffield, and I saw a restaurant that looks like it's been closed down for a long time. Maybe you should take a look at it." We had told him I had always wanted to open my own restaurant.

The morning after Rocky told me that, I put Mari in the car with me and dropped Rocky off at work so I could go and see this place. Mari didn't have a car seat because it wasn't a legal requirement at the time, so I was just holding her while I drove. People couldn't imagine doing that today, I know. I didn't have a stroller, either, so I parked the car, put Mari on my back to keep her safe, and emerged from the car to check out the restaurant.

I kind of snuck a look into the window, and this guy passed by me. "You want to open a restaurant, Chinese girl?" He actually called me that, "Chinese girl." It was the landlord, the owner of the restaurant and indeed the whole building.

"Come to my office next door."

So I followed him to his office with Mari on my back.

"I'm a very hardworking person. Do you see my hands?" And I showed him my hands. "But I don't have any money. All I have is $10,000." I was very honest with him. "And if I open a restaurant, I can't give you $10,000. I have to change the sign, and I need money for that. I have to get the different cooking equipment. How much do you want to sell the restaurant?"

"I'll only sell for $70,000."

"Oh, I don't have that kind of money. Can I see inside?"

He showed me inside. I thought, "Oh, it looks so beautiful."

"You could use everything in here," he said.

I looked at him. "I can work hard. If you give me this place, I will be able to pay you back in two years."

The first year, we paid back $40,000. The second, we paid back $30,000. That split was in our contract, and he was really nice about lending the money because nobody had wanted to lease the place. Because of the lack of interest shown by others, he also gave a rental rate much cheaper than expected, although it was expensive for us at the time, $1,400 a month.

Restaurant leases don't usually have to pay the property taxes, and after the first year it became his responsibility to pay our water bills, so I was satisfied with our operating expenses from the beginning. And he gave us a long lease, 10 years with an option to renew.

It was such a good lease, I asked him how many restaurants he had, and he said, "Oh, only one restaurant."

After I signed the lease, I went to the Italian seafood restaurant around the corner, which is no longer there.

"Hi, I'll be coming here a lot now, because I'm the new owner of the restaurant around the corner!"

"Oh, do you know how many restaurants have gone through there?" He asked.

"Well, do you mean there was more than one?"

"You're the fourth person!"

I laugh about it now, but I thought, "Oh my god!"

I don't know if I finished my dinner or not, but I don't think so. I came home and told my father.

"Wow, this is going to be the fourth restaurant there. How am I going to do this?"

I don't know if it was my mother or father who said, "It all depends on the management and how you take care of the place, so don't worry..."

But really I had no choice. I had signed the lease, even if there was no way I would have if I had known four restaurants went there then closed down.

Still living in that $230 apartment, we had to come and start painting the rooms of the restaurant, change the stove, do everything ourselves. Somehow it went very smoothly. Even my mother was being very nice. At that time, it wasn't even as hard to get a liquor license in Chicago, as it is these days. I applied for the liquor and food licenses at the same time, though, and we did get the food license first.

But we had to open without a liquor license because we ran out of money.

In days before the restaurant opened, we only slept, like, three or four hours a day. It was the summertime, and we needed to get ready to open. While we did this, our apartment was always piled high with laundry.

One time we went back to the apartment and the toilet had backed up. We couldn't believe it, and we weren't prepared to clean it up. We just slept in the restaurant and didn't go back for two days. The smell was terrible.

We moved out of that apartment to a two-bedroom place next door to the restaurant. It was a little expensive, like $500 or $600, but we had to get out of that apartment.

There was one thing on our minds: "We've got to open the restaurant. We have to open." That was our concentration. Rocky was very supportive at the time, and I firmly believed it was wholly two people's decision. It was two people, not just mine! He's the one who found it, and I'm the one who went there.

Rocky and I got married after I got my green card. We had lived together without marrying before Mari was born for green card reasons, which were that I could not get a green card from my mom if we got married, because only non-married kids could get green cards from their parents. I got my green card after maybe two or three years of my mom and dad getting theirs, and Rocky and I got married after Mari's birth.

We opened the restaurant on July 21, 1983. Besides Rocky and me, we hired one man to help in the kitchen, and one bus girl to help me in the front.

People would come by and look at the menu in the window. As I watched them, I was very excited. I thought, "Maybe we will have customers on our first night." That night we were very busy, so busy that the kitchen helper quit. I got down on my knees and begged him to stay. It was just exhausting. We managed to sell $800 worth of food the first night. I was so happy.

The next night, only a few customers came. I was thinking, "What happened?" My dad decided to take a walk around the neighborhood. Later, he came back, and I was sitting on the stairs of the restaurant. There were only two or three customers inside. He sat down next me and said, "Dee, the other Asian restaurant only has two customers." I felt better. That was kind of the beginning of my father turning nice.

I later found out that the people walking by were going to the neighborhood garden walk, called "Sheffield Garden Walk." They had to pass by the restaurant to get to the gardens in the area, so it was very lucky for us. But from that day, the restaurant grew and grew. The first time I met with our accountant, two weeks later, I fell asleep while he was talking to me.

At times our tempers were very short. Summer can be very hot in Chicago, and one night it was so hot that the air conditioning could not cool the restaurant. We were completely full and people were waiting outside. Rocky and the helper had a hard time keeping up with the orders. I would check in the kitchen to get the customers their orders as quickly as possible.

Rocky was just really hot and tired working with the wok in those temperatures. Finally, he said in anger, "You want it; you cook it." And then the wok came flying at me. For the rest of the evening, I walked around with oil all over my clothing. Yes, everything was a struggle, and we had struggles. Still, we were happy.

But let's go back to the weekend that we opened. Finally, I had to go do laundry, because as usual it was piled up so bad. My mom and I went to a large commercial laundry at Webster and Halstead. On the way in I saw a lot of signs—this or that item "FOR SALE, you know?" I thought, "Something is going on here." I put the laundry in and after that we started to look for the garage sales in our new neighborhood. I still had my love of garage sales, and we found a lot of baby clothes for Mari. I found many things I wanted for her and paid just $40!

Ten thousand dollars was almost enough to open the restaurant, but we had to make a menu and do the buying, which meant, without a line of credit at the wholesale grocery store, that we had to pay for everything in cash. Nor would they deliver to us: we had to go pick it up, sometimes twice a day, because we didn't have a big car. With Mari and her car seat, and Rocky and me in the front, one giant bag of rice and a vat of soy sauce could pack the whole car, so we had to go at least twice.

Rocky and I set a goal for the restaurant. If we could at least make our salaries in profit, the restaurant was a success. The restaurant far, far exceeded this. In the early months, our landlord was very supportive. He even helped make cocktails at the bar after we got our liquor license. But as time passed and our restaurant became a huge success, he wanted to raise our rent. I said, "No."

It's too bad, but things between us turned very ugly. He would call me names like "Chinese Girl," you know? He would also turn our water off. For several months, we just fought, fought, fought. Then I could not take it any more, okay? All this time, I was pregnant with Eddie. The stress of fighting with him and trying to run the business was just too much. I gained seventy-five pounds. Ending the lease was my only option. But we had nowhere to go, you know?

One day a customer who is a real estate broker told me she can help. She had two buildings on Armitage Street near my current location. "At the bottom of the building, you can build out a restaurant," Barb said. I remember thinking, "I have to do this."

The loan for the building was $380,000 and the construction loan was $400,000. By this time, I was only twenty-eight years-old, but I was not afraid. I knew in my heart that this would work, so I went to Barb, and I said, "Okay, I want to do this."

We worked day and night to open the new restaurant. But things moved very slowly. The reason nothing was getting done was that the architect had not gotten the permits from the city of Chicago.

I decided I had no choice. I must get the permit myself, okay? At 8:30 a.m. one morning, I got Mari ready and went down to City Hall. Eddie had been born by then, so I left him at home with Rocky. All day, I waited. 9:30 a.m. came. No permit. 12:30 p.m. No permit. 1:30 p.m. Still, no permit. Finally, at 3:30 p.m., I gave up and went home.

When I got there, I was really tired and feeling defeated, and I went over to Eddie's crib to check on him. Eddie was laying in his poo, okay? Rocky had left Eddie in the crib all day without checking on him. So I spent two hours cleaning the crib, Eddie, and the bed sheets. By the time I finished, it was past 5 p.m. Now Rocky and I had to go to the restaurant.

The next day, I got up and prepared Eddie and Mari, and, again, went to City Hall for the permit. I waited all day, again, but finally, I got to see someone. He told me that we were over the capacity limit for seating and that the space has to be re-engineered. Well, I could not take it, you know? I broke down right in front of the inspector. All of my tears just come out. Thankfully, he felt a lot of sympathy for me and explained what I needed to do. I was so happy.

It was a very hard time for us, but the new restaurant was completed. We moved to our new location, okay? This is the location we have been in ever since.

From the beginning, the restaurant was named "Dee's Restaurant." This gave it the personal touch. We also knew that I would be the face to the customer. I really think my customers love me, and I love them. The customers always gave me joy. When I went to the restaurant, I would dress up very nicely for them every night. And when I was not there, they would always ask for me. They would say, "Where's Dee?" you know? I really found my happiness in pleasing my customers. That was the end of my day.

My day always began with me taking care of the children. Before Eddie was born, every morning, the very first thing I did was take care of Mari. Of course, I was always the one of the two of us to do this, and Mari was a very difficult girl. She cried a lot at night, and she wouldn't sleep more than two hours on end. When she couldn't sleep, we had to take her out and drive her around until she fell asleep, with no guarantee that she wouldn't wake up when we eventually had to turn back and bring her home. Mari's love of driving encouraged me to take her on errands to the wholesale grocery and the bank.

My mom took Mari to the zoo every single day. To this day, my daughter Mari won't eat eggs, because she saw the chicks hatching at Lincoln Park Zoo when she was a tiny little girl, already a completely different person from me. We think so differently that I almost imagine she is trying to say something about our relationship. Her refusal to miss a minute of the drama of the emergence of each little, tiny, completely different chick seems like a criticism of me for missing many personally significant scenes in her childhood.

And Mari is not like me. I was always sensitive to the suffering of my mother, and no matter what, I still believe, "I must honor my parents." Even from the beginning, Mari was not growing up in the Asian way of thinking. I could not easily accept her strong need for independent thinking, and it often strained our relationship.

Then there was the relationship between my mom and dad. Though they had a more comfortable life in America, they still fought a lot. It was unbearable to watch as an adult, a worse feeling than the sadness I remembered from my father's absence in my youth, when it seemed he scared my mom half to death.

Now they fought for no reason, for nothing, and they fought always. Small arguments became big fights. Every argument became a big fight. It got to the point that I was unable to see that they had ever liked each other at all.

She complained a lot of course. In Korea, my mom was always a little scared of him; then when they came to America that turned upside down.

My mom became aggressive. After they were in America, I realized this: my mom is like a cat and my father was an unfaithful male mouse grazing in a well-stocked American kitchen as though it was his own little world.

She would complain about everything. I don't know how to convey it except by repeating myself. Everything bothered her. When my father was nice to her, it bothered her. If he was mean to her, it bothered her. You know, she was just never happy. It's just... everything bothered her.

When we were in Korea, when she wasn't happy, when she had an argument with my father, she couldn't fight with my father because my father was like a king.

But she had her own way. Our home was his castle, so she went to the attic. She would take out this little container, go up there, and not come down at all for two or three days. She would just disappear. During our time at home, if we didn't see our father, he was out gambling; if we didn't see my mom, she was in the attic, and we had take care of ourselves and my younger brothers. There were too many of those days, too, too many of those days. I hated it; too many of those days.

Here in America, my mom still found things to argue with my father about. Then when she would get angry she wouldn't talk to us. She would just sleep for two, three days. Now there's no attic for her to go to, so she slept for two, three days. Gradually she woke up, you know, so that just became normal in our family. And my father became like a mouse.

Many mornings, I came to the restaurant and found my father sleeping there. I didn't tell my family that my father was sleeping at the restaurant, you know?

My mom kind of turned out to be a revenger. She would pick at everything. If nothing happened, she would pick something and get into a fight. I think she wanted to punish my father for what he did in earlier times.

But time passed quickly and soon my father was turning 71. By then, Dee's Restaurant had been in business for five years. I had learned that Chinese people celebrate certain birthdays with particular enthusiasm: 61, 71, 81, and 91. So I thought, "You know what? My father is turning 71." When my father was turning 71, all us brothers and sisters wanted to give him a huge, big party because it's so big.

We were talking about where we were going to have the party and everything, and we decided to have it at my big new house in

Glencoe. I had a huge yard, so we could have the party outdoors. We hired a band. I invited all of his friends, and I held it on Labor Day Monday.

I took my father to the store of one of my customers and bought nice shoes for him and a wonderful suit. That's the suit he took with him at his funeral. We put that suit on him, you know, okay? That suit looked incredible.

I bought my mom a wonderful dress. I spent $800 for dresses for my mom and myself. Yeah, I bought one for me, too, but my mom's was much better. I was really looking forward to this birthday party with all my brothers wearing tuxedos. It was our first big family event, and we invited our very close customers, and they came.

But my mom was like, uh...my mom. I didn't see huge, big happiness on her face. Even though she's not a very open person, I just didn't have a good feeling. Even when the pictures came back, I looked at my mom, and there was just something in there, you know?

Later on, right after the party finished, my aunt and uncle arrived. I actually invited my uncle to come from China for my father's birthday party, but their visas got kind of delayed. So right after the party was held, my uncle and my aunt came, and that's how we found out my dad had cancer.

And later on, after my father passed away, my mom said something that really made me angry. She said, "You know what? That big party we call '61, 71, 81' is huge, big party, okay? Those big parties, some people can't handle. Some people cannot handle, and your father couldn't handle: this is why he pass away."

I was just like, "Uh, it hurts me a lot. A lot. I put all my effort into that party. I'm the one who put all the money into it, because my brothers and sister, they all have a restaurant, but at that time, they're not doing as well as I am..." I was really, really top.

I was really giving my best for my parents. And I paid for the food, for the band, you know? Everything.

I wanted to give the best to my father, okay? I didn't know that he was sick.

It all began like a cold. He started coughing a lot, and his brother from China said, "I think you better take your dad in for a check-up." But usually, when you have a cold, you don't go to the hospital to get a check-up, do you? You just go to the doctor's office and take your medicine, but somehow that time I took my dad to the hospital for a check-up, and we found that the x-ray showed that there was something on his lung. Later, we knew this was cancer, and the doctor gave him about two years to live, and then...we didn't tell him.

We did tell my mom. We didn't tell my father, but he kind of knew. He kind of knew that we weren't telling him what was happening, and so every, like, two months or so we took him for radiation. I think in the beginning it was chemo, and later it was getting big, so chemo and radiation together.

That's how he lost his appetite. He couldn't eat anymore. In the beginning, it was only chemo. He was losing hair, but he could still walk around. He was still pretty good. He might be weak one week, you know, but then he would come back to his normal energy right away.

But after that, after chemo and radiation together, he just totally lost his appetite. He could not eat. He would throw up. He couldn't eat, and he couldn't stay at home because he was too weak, even though he had been a really nice, strong man. Because he wasn't eating, he lost so much weight, he was just like skin and bones, you know?

When he got a little bit healthy, strong, he wanted to come home right away. Dad would sit in the chair, and he could hardly go open the door for us if we went upstairs. He was that weak.

One time, we put him in the hospital, and I went to see him the next day. The nurse grabbed my arm and said, "I need to talk to you, okay? You're Mr. Bi's daughter, right?"

"Yes?"

"Do you know why your father is in the hospital?"

"Yeah, he has lung cancer."

"Do you know your father was smoking in the bathroom?"

"You know what? He's seventy-one years old. Let him slip, okay? Let him smoke, because the doctors say it's not worth it to do the surgery. Just let him be. If he doesn't smoke, it doesn't mean the cancer is going to go away. Just let him be happy."

So he was in and out of the hospital a lot.

Every time he went in, of course, it was getting worse and worse and worse. Because he was in and out a lot, we didn't stay there overnight with him. Usually, my mom would be the one to stay there, but she only did that sometimes. Sometimes, not. One day, he had to get an open tube installed in his body for his food, so they could send it right to his stomach, because he couldn't use the bathroom. The surgery went very well, and he was resting very well. The food was going to his stomach well.

One day, not long after the tube was inserted, I left my house for the hospital and had driven for only ten or fifteen minutes. But the weather was so bad, I couldn't see what was in front of me, you know? I was kind of hesitant: "Maybe I should not go today. Maybe I should wait 'til tomorrow. I don't have time to go now. Maybe I should wait for the next day." But somehow, that day, I just got the feeling, "Just go, just go, just go see your dad"—even with super-bad weather. All the way there, I felt like my car would go into Lake Michigan, it was so bad.

I managed to make it to the hospital, though, and it was sunny by the time I arrived. Yeah, it was a big sun, it was beautiful weather, you know, and my mom was there. My mom was able to take the bus there. My dad looked pretty healthy that day. I brought him some flowers, these purple orchid flowers he especially liked. I put the flowers down, though he didn't know they were there, and I saw my mom even cut his nails for him, and my father looked really, really good.

At the time, I was five months pregnant, with our third child, so I had a big stomach, you know? And I said to my father, "I'll be back tomorrow." I had been going every day. Somebody even said I shouldn't, one time, when my father was in intensive care. I was pregnant, they said, and the hospital was not good for me, but I didn't care.

I didn't hate my father for what he did when we were young. You know what? I was very respectful, so I honored my mother and my father, both. I never had a moment to say, "Oh, because you were not a good father, you know what? I don't care how much you're nice to me right now!" I still respected him as my father, you know, very much.

That night, I came home, and then, at 2 o'clock in the morning, the phone rang. The minute I heard the phone ring, I knew something was wrong. Usually you don't get a phone call that late. It was a doctor, and he said my father had just passed away.

I just couldn't believe my father had passed away. He was so nice during the day when I had gone to see him. He was so nice, and he looked like he was getting stronger from the food that had begun to reach his stomach after his catheter surgery. I just couldn't believe that he passed away.

We had to drive from Glencoe to the hospital. Rocky drove, and I was crying so bad the whole way there. Everybody else was there already, because I lived the farthest at that time.

My father had already passed away, but his face, he was, his body was still in the room, you know? Oh my God, my father looked so peaceful. So, so peaceful.

He didn't close his eyes, you know, yeah. I don't know who finally closed my father's eyes. I think it was my brother. I wanted to cry so bad, because that was probably the first dead person in our family since our grandparents. We weren't experienced with death, you know, so my brother and I cried the most. It got so bad, the doctor had to send me down, because I was pregnant. I was so emotional, you know? I just couldn't believe my father died.

My mom didn't cry. My mom just seemed kind of numb. She looked so strong, and by the next day, our family was starting to arrange the funeral.

The Chinese people say when the parents pass away, the children or the family have to be next to the person. We were supposed to be next to my father, but we didn't know my father was going to pass away that night. He was supposed to be coming home the next day, or a couple days later, at the most, because the tubes were going well. He was supposed to come home, and the doctor was going to teach us how to insert the tube...so nobody was next to my father when he passed away. My mother was kind of sad about that.

But anyway, we arranged the funeral, and oh, we cried so much. We picked the funeral home right by my sister, so I had to pass the funeral home every day. Even right now, when I pass that funeral home, I cry. It's just, I think about "Oh, my father was left alone there." I think about them taking my father from the room, and I feel so cold. I feel like he was so cold, and he had to go to the basement, and there is all this emotion, and you know what? At the funeral, after we buried my father, my mom cried so bad, for the very first time.

I thought that she would not cry. I thought that she was still revenging my father. I thought the whole time my mom was pretty nasty, you know, from the beginning to the end. I would have thought that she didn't care, because all their life they were fighting and arguing, and we didn't have peace among the family at home.

I was wrong. She was so left out, so lonely. She got so depressed. She got more depressed than before. I think she still misses my father. But when they were together, it was just so bad.

Surviving The American Nightmare

Eddie was born in 1985, two years after we opened the first restaurant. I remember the day he was born as being one of the happiest days of my and Rocky's marriage.

Maybe I knew that Eddie was coming that day because I worked until 4:30 a.m., making sure that everything was taken care of. Once again, I had to deliver the baby by c-section, but this time we could pay for it! Rocky arrived at the hospital from the restaurant, smelling like Chinese food. It was his idea to name the baby Eddie, after an employee from Shanghai who Rocky liked a lot.

The first night Eddie and I were at the hospital, Rocky was the perfect father. When we were in Japan, he had treated me well, but never had he held me in such high regard as he did that night. He was so happy that I had given him a son. He was looking at Eddie, looking at me. That was one happy night; I never had it with him like that before. The emotion felt like he cares about me.

There was no joy like that the night when Mia was born. Eddie was now six years old, and I never thought to have another baby. I cannot say Rocky and I couldn't have had a good life. We still had a day-to-day relationship. We still had our good times. But everything had changed a lot.

Rocky was always a very quiet man. He doesn't like to talk. Actually, the only time he talks is when he gets drunk.

So, once in a while, he liked to come home to get drunk. Sometimes, I drank with him, but most of the time, I didn't, because I had to get up the next day to take care of the kids, the restaurant, and the house.

The way we ran our house forced me to get up. In our house, to be honest, if even a light bulb burned out, Rocky didn't know it. I had to get up just because there were light bulbs to change. Problems and breakdowns were invisible to him. We had three or four cars, but I was the only one who changed the oil. One time I got scared because it had been 8,000 miles since our last oil change, Rocky didn't notice. I said to myself, "I'm going to let it go. I'm not going to do this oil change. I'm going to see if he's going to do it or not." It got up to 8,000 miles, but he would not do it. I was the one who got up and did the oil change, because if I'm on the highway, and the car breaks down, I'm the one who will be stuck. I will have to be there making all those phone calls to take care of whatever the mess is, there on the highway, and so I have to do it. If I think about it, I better just do it.

I didn't care if he helped me, because I was still building my dream. Yes, and also, it was easier for me to accept the nature of Asian men. I still couldn't tell much difference, okay? I just thought that was the way it was supposed to be.

When Eddie came, things changed a lot. There were two kids, and, man, I was just, like, totally different with two kids. I started to rub and rub and rub, and Rocky started getting more afraid, and more afraid, and more afraid. Then he started to go out more—even at nighttime, he started going out.

After I got pregnant with Mia, my blood pressure started getting so high. It may have been from the pregnancy—I was thirty-four years old, and the doctor warned me that I could not stand on my feet. They started swelling so much, the doctor said I had to keep them up, and I couldn't do that at the restaurant. The doctor said, "You don't have to work."

And it was getting so hard to work, because Mari and Eddie needed me at home. I couldn't leave those two with the babysitter all the time. With Mia coming, and my belly starting to get bigger and bigger, finally one day I said to Rocky, "Rocky, I have to be a mommy at home, okay? I cannot hire babysitters. I can hire ten babysitters, but they can't do my job as a mother. I have to stay at home and take care of the kids."

After that, we made an arrangement. I would still go to the restaurant to help pay the bills, and do a few things, and I would go to the restaurant on the weekends. Otherwise, Rocky would be in charge of the restaurant.

But Rocky didn't have the power I had at the restaurant, because he didn't help with the chores. And everyone was Chinese. So when the staff spoke in Chinese, Rocky would say, "Fucking Chinese!" He would never complain about things by-the-book, which is to let people know something is wrong right away: "Please don't do that, blah, blah, blah..." Okay? Rocky never had the power to say that. Instead, he came home and complained to me.

From the beginning, things weren't working, but I didn't realize how bad it was. Slowly, I started to find out when I came to work on the weekend. There were so many wrong things. When I went home, I would ask Rocky: "How can you let this pass? How can you let that pass? You have to say to the staff: 'you're not supposed to do this! You're not supposed to do that!" Every weekend, I would go home arguing, arguing because he didn't take care, so being a couple became very difficult. It is very difficult to be together, work together, go home together, and still be a couple. There were so many times I said to Rocky, "I cannot be like a robot, where, if you turn the switch to 'Restaurant', I'm the restaurant woman, and if you turn the switch off, I go home and turn into your wife, okay? If I have a certain feeling at work, I carry that feeling home."

Still we fit together enough that I said to him, "I cannot just cut out all my feelings. Whatever I think about when I'm in the restaurant totally connects to how I feel when we're at home. We're fighting a lot now. I think it has gotten worse since I stopped working on the weekdays, because now we fight the most on the weekends, so we don't have any peace at home, because home is the place where we talk and fight about the restaurant the most."

It was a struggle between the kids and Rocky, the restaurant and staying at home. Even after I had stayed at home for three months, even after it stretched to three years, we didn't have peace.

I felt guilty. I WAS guilty. Every time I came to the restaurant, every weekend, it generated anger I didn't want to bring home. When I was home, I worried about, "Oh, Rocky didn't do da, da, da, da." And I hated to call during business hours to make him realize what he needed to do, so I didn't talk to anyone at the restaurant unless something had happened, and they had been forced to call me.

Part of the problem was how Rocky managed his day. He liked to leave home at about noon. If I didn't fix him breakfast, Rocky would go out to get breakfast himself. After that, he went to the driving range to hit the ball. In the afternoon, he went to his friend's restaurant to eat lunch, get a Starbuck's coffee then arrive at our restaurant at 2 o'clock in the afternoon to open the door for our employees. While the employees set up the restaurant for the evening, Rocky would sit at the TV to watch the *Jerry Springer Show*. After Jerry Springer was over, he would go back to the driving range to hit more balls. Not once did he help the staff with the chores.

At about six o'clock, Rocky would finally return to the restaurant and see customers for a couple hours. At that time, we did a good business. We did group things. We had people lining up! Rocky would probably see customers until about 8 o'clock in the evening. Then he would go out, go to a bar, and start to drink.

At some point his drinking became worse, worse, worse,

worse, but he was probably doing it for a long time. All that time, I didn't know he wasn't watching the restaurant, checking the orders coming in, checking employees, checking everything, checking anything. I found all of this out much later on.

But by that time, I could feel that things were going wrong. I knew that Rocky was getting drunk too much—he got two DUIs. Yes! Oh my God. After the first DUI, he got his license back right away. Actually, I was with him for the first DUI. He didn't really drink that much, but he was driving too slowly. He didn't bump into anything or have an accident with anybody that time, so it wasn't too serious, and they gave him his license back. The second DUI was the big problem. Rocky got very drunk, and his buddies had to tell me he had been arrested. He found a lawyer, who promised him his license back in six months, but the lawyer cheated him. Rocky spent $10,000. Of course, he didn't get his license back.

Then he wouldn't listen when I told him he wasn't supposed to drive, not for the whole five years, so he drove the entire time. He must have known he would get in serious trouble if the police caught him driving under the influence again, because he started acting like he had all the more reason not to come home when he went out to drink. Some nights, he never came home.

While Rocky was playing golf, I began taking tennis lessons. I had never picked up a racket, but I had always loved those tennis skirts. I started playing because, when I joined the health club, I saw all these women wearing tennis skirts, taking tennis lessons, and they looked so cute. I thought, "Oh my God! I want to wear a tennis skirt! I better take some lessons!"

I took my lessons next to a whole bunch of kids. Eddie watched from upstairs, so one day I said, "Eddie, do you want to hit the ball?" He said, "Yes, I do," so I signed him and Mari up together. Eventually, Eddie started jumping up through the ranks to the higher-level classes, so after a year, I stopped my lessons so I could put all the money into Eddie's lessons, because he was getting so good. You could see Eddie's talent. Soon his coach recommended that he start to go out and get into tournaments.

Eddie began going to tournaments, and I was driving him from one place to another, totally focused on my son. You know Asian parents: when your kids develop some talent, you go crazy. I was there; I was crazy, too. I just thought, "My kid has talent!"

Rocky seemed happy, too, watching his son win all those tournaments. Eddie is short, but he's fast and very smart. It made us so proud when we heard people say, "Here comes Eddie Kang."

All Asian parents are focused on their kids. And I was so proud that my total focus went to Eddie, even though I was suffering inside, and Mari was left by herself most of the time.

With Mari, I focused more on her studies. I was so strict. I wanted my kids to have the best education. I wanted them to have the best at school, whatever was the best in Chicago. I wanted to give them a great education.

But while I was focused on our children, Rocky was focused on getting drunk. Then he started giving me excuses about why he could not work, and I realized our life was becoming impossible.

We were drawing apart, and I was building up anger, more and more and more. The more anger I built—anger that made me green—the more I pushed him away.

As I pushed him away, he friends would say more and more: "Hey, Rocky! Rocky, come on, let's go away now!" And Rocky would go. He would just jump in his car. Our marriage didn't seem to exist in his mind.

Later on, I found out he had more bad habits. He started going to Korean bars, the kind of Korean bars that have individual rooms. Each room is covered, so what you are doing is secret. The women can touch you, or do whatever, and nobody would know. Yeah, so he started to go there.

Those Korean bars are very expensive. If you don't have

$1,000, you don't go there. His friends loved to take him there. Why? They don't have that kind of money, so he was the one to pay the bill!

Our money was getting less and less, so I started to nag and nag and nag. The more I nagged him, the more I pushed him away. The more I nagged him; the more he drank. We started to become my father and mother.

I was nagging more; he was drinking more. I was nagging more; he was going away more. For me, it was like, "I am home taking care of the kids. You have got to be at the restaurant taking care of business!" But he wasn't doing so. I only got angrier.

Was there another way to deal with this? Not for me. That's how my mother dealt with it my whole life. My anger built up, because he was never there to be the father. He was never there to take his kids to go to the park and play ball or something. I got very, very angry that he wouldn't do that. But you know what? I didn't want to get angry all the time, so I let him do that, you know, okay? And the business started going down, down, down, down, down, down, down.

Finally, he drank more than he would come home. Before, it was like he would be home five days and go drinking for two days. Later on, it got up to seven days. Then we stopped talking.

I didn't even have the words to talk to him. There was no technique to talk to him to say: 'Let's not do it this way, okay?'"

There were questions in my mind like: "Why are you like this? I'm home taking care of the kids. It's not easy. You're never there for me, okay? We built the restaurant so good. I'm not there, so you have to take care of the restaurant. It's our business, you know?"

Sometimes I would say, "You're not like your friends or anything. You have three kids." Among his friends, there was nobody like him. No one had three young kids and a restaurant to take care of. Either they had a restaurant, and they didn't have kids, or they had a restaurant and their kids were grown up and out of the house. No one was in his situation.

But he spent the same time out at night that they did. He thought he was a single man.

The restaurant began to totally crash and burn down. We had 100 seats, and we started seating thirty people at night. Yeah, we would get thirty people. When business was good, we had 150 - 200 people on the weekend. Now thirty or forty people were the most we got. Fifty would be crazy, okay?

By that time, most of our mortgages were paid off. Everything had been paid off, so there was no pressure to make money. And we weren't making any money!

The real problem was that Rocky and I didn't have the power to change. And he didn't have the power to talk about it. His answer was to run away. He never tried to solve the problems. He always, like, ran away.

One night, he came home and said he was going to leave. "I'm going to go back to Japan," he said. "I'm going to leave around such and such a date. I'm going to go to Las Vegas for a couple days. I'm coming back here, and I'm going to pack, and I'm going to leave."

At that moment, I felt something. When he said he was leaving, I could see there was a very painful look on his face. Even though he was a little drunk, you know, I could see it was painful. I sensed something.

So the next day, I called his friend—one of his Korean friends, okay? I didn't like any of his Japanese friends.

They were so bad. They were all bad. If they could destroy our marriage, they were happy. That's my thinking.

But this one Korean friend, I had known him since he came to America, so I had known him for twenty-some years. I called him. "Kenny, I want to have coffee with you." I said, 'What is going on with Rocky? Tell me the truth. There is…—" I started to ask, "Is there a woman there?"

At first, he would not talk to me.

"Sister-in-law, I don't know what to tell you," he said.

Then I knew. Just from the words. I'm a very sensitive person.

"Brother is going to a different place for long time, and this Korean woman is here for six months on a visa. Rocky asked me to go to Las Vegas," Kenny explained.

It started to match together in my mind.

"Oh sister-in-law, the Japanese friends are giving him a huge, big good-bye party tonight. I was invited, too. I didn't tell you. I didn't know where to start to tell you. But don't worry about it. I'm going to be at the party. I will guard him. I will do that. Whatever is going on, he get very drunk, I will bring him home."

Kenny was our friend and tried to comfort me by his words. But I could not find comfort.

That night, Rocky got really, totally drunk. And Kenny brought him home as he had promised. I was already asleep when I heard the noise: BANG! It came from the front of the house. At the front entrance was Rocky, totally passed out. Though I was exhausted myself, emotionally and physically, I hauled him onto the bed, but I couldn't sleep.

I never went into Rocky's things. But that night, he gave me a sense to open his business bag—the bag he carries back and forth from the business. I got out bed, opened the bag and started digging things out.

What did I find? A fax paper to him with a reservation in Las Vegas: a hotel, four days and three nights. I think the hotel was the Four Seasons. The reservation had his name and a lady's name.

My whole body was numb. I wanted to cry; I don't have a tear come out. When Rocky drank and went out with friends, his Japanese friends, I took that because most Japanese drink. They are like that. And most Japanese men of Rocky's era are not family men. They feel that they can have a family but still enjoy themselves. They're selfish like that. I took that when I lived in

Japan. Because I know how it is, okay? But when there's another woman, I was totally numb. Because at the bottom of my heart when he was drinking, I was angry he's not a family man, but I, I still trust him.

The next day, he woke up and left me. When I drove the kids to school that day, I still had the fax paper with me. I wasn't a wise mom, either. I pulled it out in front of my kids and said, "Do you know how I feel right now? Your father is fooling around with another woman, and he's going to leave me. He's going to take this woman to Las Vegas. Here's the paper." I totally blew up in front of the kids.

I never believed that he would give money to somebody else. But I didn't know there was another woman. So all of a sudden, POW, I think about the money in our restaurant safe. I called him.

"Are you at the restaurant?"

"Yes."

"We don't have money in the bank. I have to get money to deposit to the bank. It's not enough to pay the bills," I lied. But he was nice. He trusted me, and I went to the restaurant and got the key to the safe.

There was money short, $30,000 short.

"Where is the money?" I asked. But he wouldn't tell me.

"Where did you give the money?"

"I'm working here. We don't have to talk anymore." That's what he told me.

"Okay," I said. Even today, I don't know what happened to the money. I took out the remaining money. Everything else I left in the safe. Then I gave him back the key.

On the way home, it started to snow really, really hard. It had been nice in the morning. Then it started to snow really hard. As soon as the snow started to come down so did my tears. Anger, you know, everything started to come. How could he do this to me? I felt like I'm worthless because there's another woman. I felt like I was so honest. I was so honest to this man. He was the first man I met, okay? What I did from age nineteen until today, I feel like everything is just crap now. My tears were coming down and down and down. Cars on the highway were not moving—maybe five miles per hour. I just cried. I didn't care; I was just going crazy.

I didn't want to call my friend, Ling, because I was so ashamed. I don't know why I felt ashamed, but I did. What happened to me? People always looked at me as a strong person, you know? Now, I felt like...I felt so ashamed. I didn't have anywhere to go. I didn't call my mom because I knew she wouldn't give me the best advice. Whenever I had a problem I don't call my mom, okay, I don't. So I just kept driving, I drove probably over an hour.

Finally, I passed the Peterson exit, right before Touhy Avenue on the I-94 highway. That's when a little voice told me, "Call your pastor's wife. Call Mrs. Hsie."

I dialed her number...she was home. Do you know what she said to me? She said, "My daughter, I knew you're going to call me."

My face showed that I was not happy for a long time. That day she was praying, and somehow, she felt my burden. So she didn't go anywhere that day. She was supposed to go to a meeting. Instead, she stayed at home. I called her, and she said, "I knew you were going to call me," and then she said, "Come over. I'm waiting for you."

The next day was the flight. So I said, "Okay, I'll be there." But until I made it there, my anger was unbearable. I had the flight information; I had the hotel information; I had her name; I had everything, you know? I had already started to book a flight for my kids and me to go to Las Vegas before him. And since my last name is Kang, the hotel would probably give me a key to their room, and after they were checked in, I would open the door—that was my point.

I was so angry. In the beginning, I was numb. Now, I was just angry. I said to myself: "All my good time, I gave out to you! I tried to build this up, you know!" Then I thought, "I got your flight time! If I get the key, while you are inside sleeping, I am going to open the door, and I am going to kill you in front of the kids to tell you: this is what you did to me." That was my pride.

I was just angry, angry, angry, you know? And I wasn't hiding it any longer.

Though I arrived at the pastor's house, I was still crying, crying, crying, and I told her, "I already booked the air ticket. I'm going to Las Vegas. I'm going to kill both of them!" I didn't realize it until then, but I didn't want to live anymore.

She would not say anything or tell me anything. She just let me say whatever I wanted to say. Finally I was tired, and she started to hold me, and she said, "My daughter, you are my daughter. Don't do this. God will take care of this. It's not for us to do his work."

Then she said, "Let's take this matter to God. I'm going to pray." And she started to pray.

She prayed, and I cried. She continued to pray, and I continued to cry. Later on, she started to talk in another language that I didn't understand. Through all of this, I'm just crying, crying, crying.

For a couple of hours, she prayed. Then she began to cry, too. "My daughter, you're not going to go to Las Vegas. I asked God why these things happened. And I asked God how we're going to take care of these things. Go home and say sorry to your husband. Say, you're sorry. Say, you haven't taken care of Rocky because you were too busy with the kids." She continued on blah, blah, blah, blah, blah, blah, you know?

I started thinking to myself: "There's no way I can raise my kids without their father. There's no way, even if my marriage was not perfect, I cannot raise my kids without a father."

The next day, Rocky called because he realized I took the fax paper.

"I have it at home," I said, "but before I give it to you, I need to talk to you." He was at the restaurant, but he came home.

I was by myself at the kitchen table when he arrived.

"Rocky, I am so sorry." I started cry. "Think about it, I did give a lot for this family. I don't go out like other women, go out to fool around to spend time for myself. I take care of the family. At the same time, I still have to take care of the business. Even physically I'm not there, but still I do a lot of work. But you are never there for me."

And I guess he felt guilty, too, you know, because, for once, he listened. So I continued.

"Rocky, you came from broken family. Do you want your kids to have no father? We were not totally a happy family, but we can work on it. We have the kids, and we have a good time. You were nice to me, and I was nice to you in the beginning. Now we're under so much pressure. But these kids, do you want these kids to be without their father? You cannot have your kids come from a broken family, too. I am so sorry I didn't treat you good. When you come home, I wasn't there at nighttime. I was asleep. When you tell me to cook something, I'm very frustrated. I do it, but my heart is not in it. I just cook, and I go to sleep. I'm also so busy for the kids. You're busy for your stuff. This is not good. We can't hurt these kids."

Finally I said, "I don't want you to go to Las Vegas." I didn't tell him I booked the ticket already because my pastor's wife told me not to say negative things. So I said, "Please, we can start over again, okay?"

"I will not go anyplace anymore," he said. Rocky gave me his promise.

Right away, things got better. We started to spend time together. We started having a physical relationship again. I even went to Japan with him. For fourteen years, I didn't go to Japan. I don't like it. But we took a Japanese trip together. He had already purchased the ticket because he wanted to go back. I didn't have a ticket. So I said to him, "For fourteen years, I don't take a vacation. Don't you think I deserve to go?" Everything went well for about six months.

Inside me, however, there was still anger. I just didn't show it on the outside, you know? I tried to make it seem like I was okay. He seemed to go back to normal.

The end of summer came and this Chinese symphony came to town for one night to play at the opening of the Chicago Symphony Orchestra. It was on August 31st. I had bought two tickets, but I didn't invite Rocky. I went with my niece, Li. It was a wonderful, wonderful concert. At 9:00 p.m., the concert finished, and I called the restaurant. Rocky was not there.

"What time did Rocky leave?"

"Rocky left at 8 o'clock," they said.

After taking Li home, I went right back to the highway. I didn't want to go home; I wanted to look for him. She lives in Morton Grove and the next exit from her house going south is Touhy Avenue. I took this exit because I knew the Korean clubs were on Lincoln Avenue. But before I got to Lincoln Avenue, I saw one club on my left, okay? The minute I pulled in the parking lot, oh my God, his car was there.

I don't know where I got the guts, but I went inside.

"I'm looking for my husband."

They said, "Who is your husband?"

"My husband speaks Japanese. I see his car outside. He's inside."

You can't see anybody when you're downstairs. It's just a counter. All of the rooms are upstairs: private rooms, one by one.

"My husband is here," I repeated.

"I'm sorry. I cannot let you go upstairs."

"You better get me upstairs," I demanded.

Hearing voices upstairs, I ran up and opened the door to the first room. Rocky was with a woman. In the room. There was a table with bottles of Chivas Regal Scotch Whiskey. And he was heavily drunk already.

"Rocky, come go home," I said. He started talking to me like a Yakuza. He scared me. I was so scared that he talked to me that way.

"Who do you think you are? You come up here?" he demanded.

"I saw your car outside."

"If you saw my car outside, you wait outside in the parking lot. You do not come up here and open the door," he said in anger.

"Rocky, you're very drunk. Let me take you home, okay?

I went down, feeling so stupid. I even paid the bill of $270.

As I left, I said to the manager, "Don't let my husband visit in your club anymore, or I will call the police."

"It's your job to control YOUR husband," he said firmly.

I treated Rocky so good after that. I stayed with him. I cooked. I even called him before he would come home, and I'd say, "Rocky are you going to come home for dinner tonight? What should I cook?" I did the best I could, you know? But inside, I felt helpless.

I was also still angry.

The following Sunday was Labor Day. The kids had gone away for the long weekend. It was a beautiful Sunday night, with a wonderful breeze. It was so good.

We had an outdoor pool, so I turned the music on as I drank two beers, while soaking my feet in the water.

Rocky had already arrived home that evening. He slept on the sofa now, and I slept in the bedroom.

"Your music is too loud. I can't sleep," he shouted from the couch. But I ignored him, okay? Later on…he came out. "The music's too loud."

That when I got angry. I went to the family room where he was, and I pulled his head up.

"My music is loud, but how about you? You spend your time with a lady in a private room! You promised me you're not going to do that. And now, you complain my music is loud?"

He pushed me away, and it made me angrier. I came back again.

"Tell me about her? Why do you do this again? You promised me you're not going to this kind of place anymore. I don't care you if go out to drink, but you don't go to the place where you have a woman sitting next to you, okay?"

I hit his arm, and he started getting angry. Then he got up and pushed me then he kicked me.

Rocky punched me with all of his force. I didn't know what to do, so I ran into my bedroom. Now he was shouting at me, "I'm going to kill you." And he began swearing in Japanese, talking like a Yakuza. "Argh, argh, argh, I'm going to kill."

Eddie was sick that day, and because his bedroom was far away, I wanted him to sleep in my room so that I could give him medicine that night.

With Rocky behind me, I ran into the bedroom screaming: "Eddie, Eddie, your dad's going to kill me."

He cried out, "Daddy, don't do this, Daddy, don't do this." But Rocky didn't stop beating me.

I escaped Rocky's grip and ran to the bedroom where our friend, Mashi, was sleeping. Mashi is a sushi chef and for a time, he was staying at our house. That night, he was sleeping in the maid's room. Rocky is very strong, and Mashi could not stop him. So I ran from that room, too, but Rocky continued to follow me. He cornered me near the stairs and continued to beat me and pull my hair. I don't know how long this lasted. Though Eddie was crying and Mashi was shouting, Rocky would not stop.

At some point, the police came to the door. We never locked our front door because the house is far away from the driveway. One police officer came in first but couldn't stop Rocky. Then another police officer came. It took two police officers to get Rocky off me...

They handcuffed him, took him away, and I was there just shaking.

Eddie was crying and shaking. I was crying and shaking. Poor Mashi didn't know what to do.

The police officer asked me to go to the police station to report what happened. But I wouldn't say a word. They asked Eddie. I told Eddie not to say a word. I knew that if I said anything they were going to put Rocky in jail.

"Eddie, don't say anything," I said.

Because I wouldn't say anything, they sent a social worker in to talk to me.

"Mrs. Kang, you do this, you're helping other women, too." Obviously, she could see that I had been beaten, you know? She could see my face. I had bruises everywhere.

"No, I fell. I was running, and I fell." I didn't say a word about what had happened that night.

But the police said, "No matter how you cover up, Mrs. Kang, we saw him. We saw him beating you. So that's more than enough evidence. He's not going home."

Eddie went to bed, and I sat up all night. The next day was Labor Day, and the weather turned really cold. When the police took Rocky away, he had on shorts, so I got some of his warm clothes and a blanket then went to the police station.

"He bailed himself out," the police told me.

After I came home, I saw his car was gone. I called his cell phone, and he would not answer. I called again. Finally, he did.

"Where are you?" I asked.

"I'm in a motel somewhere on Lincoln Avenue," he said.

I was scared to go by myself, so I got Mashi to go with me. We went from one motel to another until, finally, we found him.

"Did you eat? Let's go eat because we didn't eat for a couple of days." So I took him to the corner restaurant. We ate, but we didn't say anything. Although he was not supposed to go home, we went home anyway.

When we went to court, I didn't want to press charges, but the judge wouldn't agree to dismiss the case because the police saw him beating me.

I tried to say that he was not an abusive person, but it didn't matter what I said, they would not let him go. Finally, I got angry, and I felt so ashamed sitting there where everyone could hear these bad things about my family life. There were so many people. I could not take the shame, so I walked out, okay?

The judge ordered him to see a counselor.

On the following Saturday morning, Rocky and I were supposed to drive Mari back to school at the University of Illinois in Champaign-Urbana. Because Rocky got arrested, I just didn't have the energy, so Mari found a friend who could drive her. The friend lived nearby, and I dropped Mari off.

We started crying so bad on the way over there. As I left her, Mari and I were crying, and, although I'm sure her friend thought we were crying because Mari was leaving, we knew the tears were for something else.

After I sent Mari back to college, I came home. Rocky also stayed home so nobody would see him. I started to go to the restaurant, and then, about a week later, he told me to book a ticket for him. He said he wanted to go to Japan for a short time.

"That might be a good idea," I said.

It was a pretty odd time. I had a pretty uncomfortable feeling, because I was still pretty angry about what he had done to me. It was pretty uncomfortable to just face that environment every day. I thought, "The whole atmosphere is so bad at home. Maybe it's a good idea for him to go away." He asked me for $50,000, and I said, "Okay, not a problem." I also ordered his ticket.

Rocky had very weird friends. His friend's travel agency

booked the ticket for Las Vegas. If I were going to Las Vegas with another man, there's no way my friend would sell me the ticket, but his friend did. I was very disappointed about that. Whatever money they could make, they did. It didn't seem to matter that their actions would break up a family.

Later, I told Mashi that I was going to give Rocky the money. "I don't think it's a good idea to give Rocky $50,000. All he's going to do...he's going to drink it all. Every single night he's going to drink," Mashi said.

Instead of $50,000 Mashi gave Rocky $5,000 from me. He wasn't mad, I heard, but I also made sure he couldn't find me before he left.

He also didn't call or anything, so I got...I was very shocked.

When I went to the restaurant that week, I had to put on a smiling face. That was so hard. And the business was so bad. After paying everything we owed. I had $700 left.

I'm not kidding. I made $700, okay? That's how bad the business was. With only $700 in my hands, I wanted to cry, but there were no tears.

Before I had, like, $70,000 sometimes. That was the peak time, but with $700 in my hands, I thought, "I don't know, I don't have the energy to move on. But, I cannot just close down. I have so many people who have worked for me for a long time. I cannot just say, 'Hey just go home and just lock the door.'" Besides I needed... I still needed the income. I also needed to cry. But there were no tears. I just didn't know what to do.

I got depressed, really, really bad. I ate like crazy. I would eat, like, a whole pot of soup, and then I would drive. In the morning, I would drop Mia at school, then drive to Dominick's, or someplace, grab a cake, go home, and eat the whole thing. Afterwards, I went to sleep. I would sleep, and then I'd get up, take a shower, pick up Mia, go back home, and that's it. I could barely put food on the table for the kids to eat.

After Mia went to bed, I would wake up, wondering to myself, "How should I do this?" There were a hundred ways I could think about it, but there's nothing you can do when the business is slow. I just felt so much pressure.

Finally, I called my niece. I have a very nice niece, Li, who left me a message saying, "Auntie, I haven't heard from you." I called her back and said, "Li, I need something. I need to talk to you about something, okay?"

"I've got a problem Li. He left here. Rocky left here, and he beat me so bad. I'm very hurt. I'm hurting so much, I don't have a face to go to the restaurant right now." She was working for a different restaurant.

"I hate to ask you to come work for me, but I really need your help. I cannot just close down the restaurant. I really need your help. Will you help me until I figure out what I'm going to do with the restaurant?"

The restaurant was now in need of repair; the kitchen tile was coming out. There was always a problem, every single day.

"Auntie, whatever you want me to do, I will help you."

"Okay," I said. "I want you to quit there, and come help me until I figure out what I'm going to do, okay?"

She was really nice, and she gave one-week's notice there. Then she came to help me.

Having Li's help made things better, but it also made things worse, because I totally stopped coming to the restaurant. Then I became more depressed.

That's when my niece and I started to go through the business records of the restaurant, looking at the invoices. I learned that we were overpaying for many things. For example, one can of soy sauce is $22, and we paid $27.50. And the carryout bags, if you use the white ones, which we did, five hundred are like $55. Well, the brown ones are $20.

At the same time, a new restaurant depot opened up. They

sent me a free card, so I went there one time to compare prices with the suppliers we'd been using. I shopped there one time, and I couldn't believe it. I could save two, three hundred dollars!

Then I said, "You know what? Somehow I've got to encourage this business to bounce back, and encourage myself."

So I tried to move on. At the same time, Rocky didn't call me. I did the best I could every day. I didn't know when he was coming back; where he was spending his time; and I had no idea where he was.

I started doing my own buying at the restaurant depot. It was a very funny feeling. For all those years, I never had to go out to do the buying. I always had it delivered to me. My thinking was, "I'm the owner; I don't go out to buy, okay?"

At the restaurant depot, to be honest with you, when I went out to do the first buying, I was scared somebody would see me. The face, you know? Do you know about saving face?

I went early, or at least tried to go at a time I wouldn't bump into somebody I knew. It was so funny that I got that kind of feeling.

But doing my own buying helped a lot. The second month of running the restaurant by myself was October, and it got a little better. I didn't save more than a thousand dollars, but I could tell things were getting better.

I tried to come into work because Li was working for me five days a week. I felt like I had to come into the restaurant on weekends and one weeknight. I was tired, so it was hard to work four days, but I tried.

It was hard to go to work and it was hard not knowing where Rocky was. As October turned into November, the weather was getting bad, and I worried about him, because he didn't take winter clothes when he left.

"He's going to get cold. He's going to get drunk. He doesn't have warm clothes. Who's going to do the laundry for him?" I started to worry about all of that.

Mari started coming home from school a lot, and she noticed I was not doing well. I remember so many nights that I barely cooked something for Eddie and Mia to eat. Eddie was really like a father and mother for Mia at that time. Before Rocky left, Eddie started getting bad. Now, Eddie started to gradually return to being nice.

There were lots of nights I was on the schedule to work, and I told Li I was going to come to work, and, after cooking something for Eddie and Mia and putting it on the table, I told them, "I'm going to work, you know? Okay?" I got in the car and said to myself, "I'm going to go to work," and a song came on that Rocky and I used to listen to together, and my tears came, and I couldn't drive. I would get so full of emotion that instead of going to work, I turned around and went home.

You should have seen me during that time! Everyday, my eyes were like a goldfish. I cried so much: day and night. I drove, and I cried. I probably barely had the energy to drop off my kids at school. I was so, so sad, so, so emotional.

I had to cry a lot to get all the tears out. By the time I finished, I didn't have the guts to go to work. I could see what my face was like. My eyes were just so puffy. I was so scared to walk into the restaurant like that I would just go home.

When I went home, Eddie and Mia would both be surprised. They could always see that I had been crying; they would hug me, and say, "Mom, it's okay. It will be okay." We hugged together, crying, crying, crying.

There were just so many nights like that. When I finally got to the point of being able to make it to the restaurant some days, my face would be swollen and Li would say, "It's okay. You can go home. I'll take care of things here."

I was so sad, so lost, without knowing where Rocky was.

Finally, in early December, I got a phone call. Rocky said he was coming back the next day, because he was only allowed to stay in Japan for three months without a special visa, and he had been there since September. I was kind of happy, and also kind of scared, because the way he talked to me was very cold.

I went to the airport to pick him up. Since it was an international flight, he had to go through immigration, so I gave him thirty minutes in my planning. I got there forty minutes after his scheduled landing, but I didn't see him. I waited and waited, but he had come out so early that he had had time to get drunk. I waited there a long time, but I never saw him, because he had gotten impatient and taken a cab to our house.

When I got home from the airport, Rocky was there, already asleep. I knew he was totally drunk, because the whole room smelled like alcohol. He woke up, but we didn't say anything to each other.

We didn't have a lot to say later, either, in the weeks since his return. I was going to work as much as possible, because I was trying to take care of the restaurant, and he stayed home. He didn't want to come into work, so he didn't.

Every night, he wanted to drink, so he did. He would speak very coldly, in the Yakuza way, which sounds threatening, like "Don't bother me," so I couldn't have a conversation with him at all. The kids were living with that, okay?

One night, Rocky wanted to talk to me. He said he needed money. He had reconnected with his stepmother while he was in Japan, and she was in crisis, and needed to borrow $80,000 "Otherwise," he said, "She cannot make it through the New Year."

"We're having problems in our marriage, and your stepmother is coming to you? This is the stepmother who threw you away! She didn't take care of you! And she's coming to us to borrow $80,000? No."

"You have to give me the money!"

"I can't."

"If you don't, I'm going to put a knife to your throat."

"Okay, okay," I said, "Okay. Let me think about it, okay?" With the way he had been, so cold, and threatening, talking and behaving in that Yakuza way, I was starting to be very scared of him.

"If I give you $80,000, you will go back to Japan!"

"Yes, I will go, but only to drop off the $80,000. Then I'll be back."

"Do you promise me?" I said.

"Yes."

"$80,000! He will be back. It should be okay. Let the money suffer," I decided.

So I went to get a cashier's check. I made it out for $80,000, and Rocky took it to Japan. I ordered his ticket, and, in fact, he did only go to Japan for that one week, to drop off the money. I thought that everything would be normal after he came back, but actually, it wasn't.

Rocky still didn't talk a lot. He didn't talk Yakuza anymore, but he was still very, very cold, just as if I was invisible in front of him. He didn't care. He didn't come to work. I kind of tried to push him by saying things like, "Oh, today I'm busy with the kids, you have to go to work," but I found out he would just sit at the bar. A couple of hours later, he would leave. Sometimes, he would come into the restaurant, get the money then just leave.

So I kind of sensed, "there is something definitely wrong, really wrong," but the New Year was coming. New Year is the biggest holiday, so I didn't make a big deal. I said, "Rocky, it's New Year's Eve, New Year's is coming. Let's go out to the Japanese grocery together." He went with me then we went home. Of course, the restaurant was open on New Year's Eve, so I had to come to work, and he even came to work with me. He didn't say much. But everyday, he tried to pick up on something to gripe about, but I didn't let him pick on me. I was just nice to him.

Traditionally, on New Year's Eve, we wait for the countdown as a family, okay? Mari wasn't home—she had gone to Champaign for a Christian Conference winter retreat or something. Mia and Eddie were home, though, so after we got back from the restaurant for the night, I started preparing a meal for us. I said, "Rocky, can you help me cook this?" I did the preparation, the washing and chopping, and he did the cooking. While he cooked, I noticed he was already drinking a lot. Then he started to swear, just trying to pick on things.

Eddie was sitting on the sofa watching television, waiting for the countdown to come in ten or fifteen minutes. All of the sudden, Rocky threw the pot he was using. He went ove to Eddie.

"Eddie, I want you to kneel down. Kneel down!"

He didn't really pay attention to his father. Watching television and talking at the same time, he said, "What is it? I'm watching the countdown."

Rocky got pissed off. "Eddie, kneel down."

Eddie sensed the seriousness in his father's tone.

"Okay, okay, daddy," and kind of kneeled down on the sofa.

"No, you get on the floor to kneel. Do you know, in Japan, when the father says kneel down, you've got to kneel down right away? You can't even put your head up."

Eddie did it, okay? I told him to do it, so Eddie kneeled down, but then he started to say stupid things. In the Japanese way of doing things, nobody talks back to their parents, you know? You respect your parents. Rocky shouted at him.

"You are a terrible son. You don't respect me. I tell you to kneel down, you don't even look in my face!"

Then I said, "You know what? Eddie says sorry, okay? Eddie, say you're sorry, and go to your room now, okay?"

He said sorry and started to walk upstairs. Just then, Rocky started picking on me, accusing me of fooling around with a man, saying I had probably been fooling around with Mashi.

"How many times have you guys slept together?"

But Mashi was right there!

"Mashi, did we sleep together? Mashi respects us so much, okay? No, no! Mashi, tell him!"

But Rocky was totally drunk. He was just trying to pick on somebody, saying more and more outrageous things, like "You've been sleeping with this guy for a long time," almost making growling sounds with his mouth. Finally, Rocky was making me so mad.

"No, I did not! I've been married to you all these years! The only time we're not together is when I take a shower! Honestly, besides when you go to work or take a shower, we're not together, but we are always, all the time, together! Are you crazy? What are you talking about? You must feel so ashamed."

Mashi was right there. He is such a quiet man. He didn't defend himself or anything.

"Mashi, tell Rocky we didn't sleep together. Tell him there's nothing going on," I demanded.

But he didn't. It made me feel very uncomfortable, Mashi kept silent while Rocky got so angry. Then Rocky started to say these stupid things, using his harshest, growling voice. I kind of sensed he was going to hit me again.

Rocky started going back to the bedroom to change clothes. Then he said something that sounded like growling sounds. Eddie kind of watched from the stairs, because the last time his father talked that way to me, he punched me, so Eddie didn't go upstairs. Mia was sleeping, so I quickly went upstairs, took Mia, grabbed Eddie's hand in mine, and we zipped outside, all three of us without shoes. I had no coat. We drove away before Rocky could put his hands on me.

It was one or two in the morning, I can't remember. I think it was not quite 2:00 a.m. I had nowhere to go. I didn't have any money, just the car and my keys, no shoes, no coat, so I went to my mom's house.

I didn't know my mom had a guest at home. One of the ladies who used to rent an upstairs room from her had come to visit her from Taiwan. When I opened the door, my mom kind of sensed something was wrong. She and her guest were talking in the living room, so she told me to go into the spare bedroom right away. Eddie, Mia, and I slept in there. I was so tired; I actually fell asleep.

The next day, I woke up at 7:00 a.m. or so. I didn't say anything to my mom. I woke Eddie up. I woke Mia up. I said, "Let's go home."

When we got home, Rocky and Mashi were still sleeping. All the things we were supposed to cook were still laid out on the kitchen island, so I put on an apron and started to cook. Why did I start to cook after all of that? I guess because I am an Asian woman. Actually, I woke Mashi up to help me with the cooking.

We cooked so many things and set them on the table. I asked Eddie to go tell his dad to come and eat, but Eddie wouldn't go. I think Mashi went to wake Rocky up.

He came out, and Mashi was sitting there, Eddie was sitting there, I was sitting there. It was a long table, and we always made a special fuss about Rocky having his own special chair, his bowl, and his chopsticks, because he was the head of the house. He sat down, and I passed the rice over to him, and the soup, and he took his chopsticks and stuck them in the middle of the rice bowl. I knew something had just gone wrong. Rocky announced, "I can't eat this kind of food." So nobody ate. I had a lot of things on the table. I can't remember if Mashi ate, but I didn't, and Eddie didn't eat.

Rocky told Eddie to go away. "Get out of this house." New Year's Day 2001 was a very, very cold morning. I said, "Come on, let's eat, okay? Let's eat." Rocky said, "No, if you don't get out of the house, I won't eat," and Eddie was like a teapot with steam coming out. Finally, Eddie said, "Okay, I'll get out of the house, okay?"

Eddie went up to the garage door, and I followed. "Eddie, go to Joe's," his friend's house across the street. Go to Joe's house for a little bit, okay? I will get you right away," so Eddie left, and I came back.

I thought, "Rocky will eat now," but no, he stuck the chopsticks down in the middle of the rice bowl again and said, again, "Who's going to eat this kind of food?" So I didn't eat. Nobody ate, okay? Nobody ate, and Rocky went back to the bedroom, changed his clothes, and left our home.

After Rocky left, I went to get Eddie right away, because it was such a hugely cold day.

"Eddie, come home, come home! Daddy's not home, okay?" Later with Eddie on one side and Mia on the other, I held both of them. The television was on, and our eyes were on the television, but our minds were somewhere else. All three of us couldn't talk about anything. Nothing could come out of our mouths. We were just kind of stunned, sitting there, I don't know for how long.

Rocky came home, I guess he went out to eat somewhere, and after he came back, he saw Eddie and me and Mia sitting there. He saw Eddie was sitting there. He said, "You don't leave, I leave..."

That's why he left, he said: because Eddie didn't leave, and then he packed up and left the house.

I thought to myself, "Did Rocky really just do that? He did. Yes, he said it was because of Eddie, so he's just totally picking on him. He tried to; he tried to leave. I guess he just didn't have a good reason to do that, so, so he said that."

After he left, he would call me on the cell phone asking for money.

I wouldn't give him money, and I told the staff at the restaurant not to give him any, because I wasn't making that much money, and the business was suffering. I had already given him $80,000. When he called me to ask for money, he talked to me really bad. I said, "I don't have the money. You know the restaurant suffers so much." Later I found out he had rented an apartment at the New Yorker. Before that, he was getting drunk, drunk every single day, and the people he was drinking with were so happy because he had some money in his pocket, and he wouldn't come home. I noticed that the only time he called me was if he needed money.

I left home, too, in a manner of speaking, but it was to take care of the restaurant. Still, leaving home meant leaving the kids—poor kids, going through those crazy things.

Finally, one night, Rocky called and said he wanted to talk to me. He said he would come to the restaurant. I was so scared he was going to hurt me. I had his friend, Kenny, sitting next to me. When he came to the restaurant and saw that his friend sitting next to me, he didn't say a word. He left without looking in my face, and from that point, he never looked in my eyes directly, not even once.

Finally I called Rocky and said, "This is not right, we need to sit down. Let's separate a little bit, okay?"

During the time I waited to have a talk with him, he used all these credit cards to go to Jamaica and Atlanta and charge, charge, charge. I could not cancel his credit card, because we were together, so he was spending all that money, and I was home, suffering, paying the bills.

One day, I was dreaming somebody was killing me. I was scared; I was sweating. All of a sudden, I opened my eyes. Eddie was taking a nap, too, on the sofa. Oh my God, when I opened my eyes, I saw this man. Bleeding. His face was totally covered with blood. Blood, blood, blood. The clothes were covered with blood. Standing in front of me was Rocky.

"Oh my God, what happened to you?" He said he fell. "Come, sit down. Let me clean you up."

I used a towel to clean up everything I could, and then I noticed the open wound on his nose. It had not been broken, but cut. There was so much blood coming out, it had run all over his body. I had to change all of his clothes.

Later on, I found out he had had a fight with his friend. Rocky knocked his friend's teeth out, and his friend knocked him in the nose and knocked him out. The friend just left him there on the ice, and when he woke up, he took a cab home, okay?

So I changed his clothes for him and everything. I treated him like a little baby, you know? I washed him up, did everything, and then he stayed home. I cooked for him every day. He stayed home, and then he was nice, a little bit nice. He was smiling a little bit with the kids. I thought, "He's coming home for good. It's good."

Rocky stayed home probably for ten days, so for ten days, I thought, "It's getting better, you know?"

And then one day, I said, "Rocky, I have to go do the buying. Are you going to come with me?"

"No, I want to stay home," he said.

"Okay, why don't you stay home. I'll go do the buying, and I'll do extra errands so I can come home and cook for you. Mia will be home at such and such a time, okay?" And he said okay, you know?

So after I did the buying and everything, I came home. I actually tried to be home early.

He was gone.

Although Rocky had said before that he wouldn't want to do business in Japan, apparently he wanted to live in Japan and do business there now. I tried to make things smooth.

"Rocky, you know our home, a couple of million dollar house, is all paid off. How about we get a home equity loan, and you take $200,000 to go to Japan and see if there's any business you can do. Then, when you need more money, we can get more, okay?"

"That's a pretty good idea," he said.

So he agreed to that, so we got a home-equity loan.

"Rocky, maybe we should get $400,000."

So we got a loan, and the interest was really, really cheap. We had one house in Morton Grove together. It was a house I bought for my mom to live in, only she didn't want to live in it—but this is another story I can tell you.

But anyway, that house had a mortgage, a very high interest mortgage, so I said to Rocky, "Maybe we should get $400,000. With $200,000, we'll just pay off that mortgage, and the other $200,000 you can take to Japan."

On the day we signed the loan, Eddie was in the car with me. In the parking lot, Eddie saw Rocky and said, "Hi Dad! Dad! Dad!" Rocky didn't look at Eddie. He just went inside the bank. I remember it was really, really painful, and then I had to sit next to him signing all these papers so they would release the loan. When Rocky got the loan, he came out, didn't say one word to me, and drove away in his car.

One day, I got a phone call from Mashi's sister-in-law. Mashi is Rocky's best friend's brother, so that means I got a call from his best friend's wife.

"Dee, what is going on with you and Rocky?" she said.

"Well, he wanted to start a business, so I gave him money, and he went off to Japan, and I'm here alone to take care of everything."

"Do you know he swore at me today? Do you know he's living with a woman?"

"I don't know anything. He never called me, okay?"

"Well, Mashi's father passed away, and my husband invited all the friends who came to the funeral, for help or blah blah blah. So Rocky was coming, too, and then Rocky called me and said, 'Can I bring somebody there?' It was his girlfriend. I said, 'No! You know you're not divorced, and our hearts are still heavily with Dee, so this is not a good time to bring your girlfriend, okay?' So Rocky went to the dinner without the girlfriend, but at the table, he started to swear at me. 'You're a stupid woman.' 'Do you know who you are? You're just a stupid bitch.'"

Rocky swore at her so bad because she wouldn't let him bring the girlfriend.

"Finally, my husband stood up and said, 'you are not even worthy of me punching you. Just get out of here.' So that's it. The friendship is finished. Rocky left. Dee, he swore at me so much, and he's living with a girlfriend!"

I decided to send Eddie away because Eddie was just being so difficult. We were bumped together so bad. Eddie had all this emotion, I had all this emotion, and we couldn't go anywhere. I threw my feelings to Eddie and Eddie threw his to me.

One day it was so hard. I remember one day, I was taking Eddie to school, and I looked so bad. My whole face was swollen. I was just sitting there, and my tears just came. I was totally depressed. Eddie said something that made me angry. I don't know how it started. I was supposed to take him to school, and he said he wouldn't go. He was fourteen, so he was pretty strong, but somehow I pushed him to the car and drove as far as Green Bay Road.

"I don't want to go to school!" he said.

"I want you to get into that school."

He wouldn't listen to me. As I was driving, he opened the door and jumped out of the car! Yes, yes, with Mia in the car, crying! He started to run away, and I couldn't even catch him, because I was in the car.

I gave up. I came home and called his advisor.

"I just had a big argument with Eddie, and he just jumped out of the car. I'm not sure if he's going to go to school or not. If he goes to school, can you please just call me and let me know?"

Thirty minutes later, his advisor called me and said, "Eddie made it to school, but he's not talking at all."

Eddie went through so much. He is a really good tennis player, but he couldn't play tennis anymore. Every tournament he went to, he lost. He just didn't have the guts to play. He still went to every tournament, even though I couldn't take him to the tournaments anymore. His coach started to take him to his tournaments. Every tournament he went to, he lost in the first round.

"Eddie, why do you do this?"

"What do you expect me to do? You guys are putting me through hell."

When he said that, I didn't have any words to say. I felt like, "I am suffering so much, and here my son is playing. I guess he knows it's not my fault, but he still has nowhere to go, so it's up to me." Finally, that summer, I said, "I have to send him away a little bit."

Mari was just left by herself. Since she was away at school, Mari didn't seem to suffer as much, but obviously she did, because she had no contact with her family. I couldn't make a single phone call to her because I was depressed.

Eddie went to China with this group, a program for finding your roots in the Shandong Province. He went to China for seventeen days or so. After he came back, I found out he had bought a BB gun, or rather a paintball gun. I didn't usually go upstairs to his room, but that day, I don't know, I just felt like it was a nice day or something, so I went upstairs. I started looking through his stuff. What scared me was finding this gun. I got so shocked because, excuse me, I didn't know what kind of gun it was. I found this gun, and I was, like, numb. I took the gun downstairs, and as I was sitting there, numb, in the kitchen, and unexpectedly, Rocky came home.

"Do you know, do you see, I found this in your son's room, okay? Look at it, okay? Aren't you the father? Look at what your son is doing because of what is going on with you and me. Look at it. This is in your son's room I found this."

Rocky didn't say a word. Then he said, "I want you to give me a divorce, okay?"

"No, I won't give you a divorce. You wish I would give you a divorce." I got so mad.

He just left.

That was sometime in August 2001. Then September 11

came. I didn't want to give him a divorce, but he had been spending crazy on the credit card. I was paying all of it, and the anger was starting to build up.

At that point, I knew he was not going to come back. Then my anger started, and frustration started to come out, as well as sadness. All the hard work I did, and he was living with another woman. I didn't want to give him a divorce, but at the same time, I had so much anger.

Mia was going to Christian school at the time. I had switched her from Glencoe Public School to the Christian school before any of this happened. Mia was starting fourth grade when Rocky left. I think God was really watching Mia. The Glencoe school was very little, so whatever Rocky did to me was all over the Glencoe newspaper, all over the Pioneer Press, so the whole North Shore knew, okay?

When Rocky punched me the day before Labor Day, the Pioneer Press came out on Thursday, so it was all over the newspaper, I didn't even have the guts to look at it. Eddie had already started school, his freshman year, so he came home and said, "Mom, some friends made a joke about dad."

"What did they say?"

"'how did your dad punch your mom?' 'Where did he punch your mom?'"

"Eddie, just ignore that."

So Eddie had a lot of pressure on him.

On that day in September, when Rocky came home to ask me for a divorce, I said, "You wish!" But I started to talk to some friends. There was a friend from Mia's school, a woman who was becoming a friend to me: Judy. She was Christian, and she saw something was going on with me. I kind of shared the story of what happened with Rocky with her, and she always gave me very, very good advice. Even though she was a Christian woman, she said, "Dee, you don't have to deal with this, you know? Just give him a divorce. Just get a divorce. You have to protect yourself. You better go talk to a divorce lawyer and blah, blah, blah."

And it was so funny...if you haven't gone through this, you probably don't know the emotions I was going through when Rocky left, and when he asked for a divorce. During that time, sometimes I felt like I wanted to open my mouth and tell everybody what it was I was suffering, okay? What I was going through and all. But sometimes, my mouth was as tight as a zipper that had been zipped up. I didn't want to say a word, okay?

So one time, I was sharing this story with one Asian woman, okay, a Korean woman. I was telling her what was going on. You know, what he did to me. "He punched me, blah, blah, blah." But this woman, "give me a sense of what the big deal is? Your husband just punched you once, you know?" When she gave me that response, it made me feel, like, you know, this was nothing. So obviously there are a lot of Korean women living that way, and after I sensed that, I didn't share the story with Asian women anymore.

But I did talk to my church mom a lot. When everything was going on, when anything went on, I just called her, and she always prayed with me. She always gave me the best advice, but at the time, I still didn't feel like I could hold onto God. You know, "God is far away, and I need somebody right next to me. I don't feel God is right next to me, okay?"

So Rocky was asking me for a divorce, and I was saying I wouldn't give him a divorce, but I shared the story with Lisa, my neighbor. One night, Lisa took me out for a walk. Lisa took me for walks a lot, and I told her, "The best walks are when there is moonlight. The Chinese have a moon festival, and we always go out for a walk on that night."

"Lisa, Rocky is asking for a divorce, you know?"

"Oh, Dee, you better start talking to a lawyer, okay?" She told me her next-door neighbor, a person I knew, too, was a lawyer.

"She's a very tough woman lawyer. Maybe you should ask some advice from her."

Later that night, the tough lawyer woman neighbor called me. "Dee, what is going on?" She was very friendly.

"Oh, you know what he did to me?" and blah, blah, blah, blah, blah. I talked for probably a couple of hours with her. "Thank you so much. You've helped me, okay? You know, thank you, so much, you know, okay, for your call." Blah, blah, blah, blah.

And I thought it was just a neighbor calling me to comfort me, and later on I got the huge big bill.

But anyway, I know this lady from downtown Glencoe, okay? A very nice lady named Hannah. I bought a coat for Rocky from her place, so she knew me, and one time I was going to Einstein Bagel. And I saw she was inside, so I went inside and said "hi."

"Dee, I am a very professional lady. You don't have to tell me, but I know something is going on with you." She just came out like that.

"Yeah, my husband has asked for a divorce. I am living pretty bad, okay?"

"Oh, Dee, I had this one woman who came in. She lived in Highland Park, and she's going through a divorce, and she went through hell with the first lawyer, but the second lawyer is supposed to be really, really good. This lawyer worked with her the way she wanted."

"Well, maybe you want to find out the name for me?"

"Dee, I'll find out the name for you right away.

So I left, and one day later Hannah called me with this lawyer's name. "Dee, you probably should go see this lawyer, okay?" I said okay, called the lawyer, and made an appointment. Later I understood this lawyer used to come to my restaurant, so I was so ashamed to have to go talk about the divorce and all that.

"Dee, I'm Barry Jacobson," he said. He has a huge, big firm in downtown Chicago next to the State of Illinois Building.

He was really nice, and, I was crying the whole time. I told him everything.

"You have to protect yourself, Dee. I encourage you to file for a divorce, but you can cancel anytime."

At that moment, I agreed with his encouragement, but at the same time I had this guilt, as a Christian. A Christian cannot get a divorce. God is not happy with divorce. But that wasn't quite the case, was it? I also felt the weight of the Asian community. Asian women suffer the burden of divorce no matter who is to blame. The Asian community doesn't accept divorce. So for me, this was not a convenient decision like it is for many Americans. This was a burden on my family and a shame on my face.

I thought, "Well, you can get divorced, but God is not encouraging you to do it." I still had my spiritual mom and dad saying, "Don't get a divorce."

But Rocky was abusing my children and abusing me. He also had a mistress.

One day I went to the cemetery for my father. I cried so much there. I also visited Rocky's parents' grave. Although they died in Japan, he moved their graves here and bought a huge, eight-person lot to carry their little bones, because that's the job you have if you intend to properly honor your parents in Asian culture. When I visited the Kangs' grave that day, I saw fresh roses sitting there, and I realized Rocky was back in America.

So I called his cell phone. I heard a woman answer the phone on the other side, speaking only Japanese, no English. I told Mari to call her father, to make sure I hadn't made a mistake, afraid as can be that I hadn't, and again the Japanese-speaker answered, and then I realized it was Rocky's girlfriend.

Next, the wife of a friend of his, an older friend I do not like, called me and said, "You guys got a divorce?"

"No, we are not."

"But you must know he brought a girlfriend to America."

"Is he taking her everywhere?" She said yes.

Even though I was talking to her, I felt like a nothing.

On the outside, I talked like, "Oh, you know there is nothing I can control", but inside, my heart was really hurting, really crying, really, really bad.

Whatever he did in Japan, I didn't see, but he was now in America, and he was going to all his friends' restaurants. I felt like I had no face. I didn't know why, but I felt like the loser.

I filed the divorce first, then told my spiritual mom. Actually, Mr. Jacobson filed it for me, and after he filed, I think Rocky had thirty days to respond.

Not long after, probably about a week or two later, I had to go to this Christian magazine shop to pick up some old Chinese Christian magazines. There is a magazine called *Christian Life Quarterly*, and I had to pick up a lot of them for my niece's mother, who was going to Atlanta for a reunion of friends, none of whom was a deep Christian like her, which is why she wanted to give copies of *Christian Life Quarterly* to whoever made it there. Only she didn't know how to get to the store, exactly, since she only knew the places she drove past in between Chicago and Morton Grove, and it was in an office building that was essentially in a field among the hundreds of office parks that surround the city. My niece had been sharing this with me.

"Auntie, I don't have time to pick up the magazines for my mom. Do you know where this place is?"

"Yeah, I know the place, and I even know the people there. I'll go pick them up for you." Sure, it was the least I could do.

So I went to this magazine place, and I don't know if there was just a strong power wanting me to share my story right there, right away, but when I went inside, a man and woman, the president of the magazine and his wife, who was also his volunteer, neither of whom I had met before, got me to start sharing my story right away. "Yeah, I came in here for a long time, I live in Glencoe and own my own business, and I'm a Christian. Right now, I'm going through an awful divorce..."

While I was talking to them, another sister came in with a box of some kind of fruit or sweet, and a tiny vase of flowers. The sister sat down and started to listen to me talking to the husband and wife, but the minute I talked about filing for divorce...this woman jumped up right away, and said, "No! You can't get a divorce! God doesn't like it."

The wife told me, "Don't worry, I know you are going through a lot, but go home and make it work. God DOESN'T like divorce. You know what you have to do: go home—don't rush yourself—think about it." And then she said, "I don't know why I came in here today. I wasn't supposed to come, but I was just picking some fruit, and I thought I would bring some in for snacking, so I just walked in, and you were here, sharing your story, and now I'm saying to myself, 'God has to be sending me to you.'"

She kept talking, and I started calming down.

"Go home, take time to think about it, and just don't get divorced, okay? Then again, even if you must get divorced, let it come from him. You don't file first, okay?"

So I went home, and it started to bother me day and night. "Oh my God, I filed for divorce! This is not right, this is not what God likes me to do." The divorce was already going pretty fast. They were starting to talk right away. Every minute, there was something.

Mr. Jacobson had handed the case to one of his assistants, Leon. He was really nice. Finally, I made a decision and called him.

"I know you are going to hate me, but I am going to let you know: I am going to take back this divorce. I want to pull back."

Leon was really shocked. "I am here to protect you, and you are not protecting yourself. How can you expect me to protect you?"

"Leon, if I have you file for divorce for me, then you can protect me that time, but now I want to cancel this. I am a Christian lady.

I have to listen to what God tells me. I have to listen to that voice in me."

"If you are not comfortable, Dee, as we talked about in the beginning, you can cancel anytime."

So I pulled back.

The next week, I was taking my son Eddie out someplace, tennis or something, and this car blocked my driveway. It wouldn't let me go, and then a man came out and served me with papers for the divorce.

My attorney called me and said, "Dee, I got the papers, too, and you are going to come in."

I went in there, and I asked him, "What if I still don't want to get a divorce?"

"If you don't give him a divorce, you can extend it, you can waste more money, but you will still pretty much end up in divorce. Every minute we talk, there is money involved, and you may still be in divorce three years later if he doesn't file for child custody, but does file for some money."

I just couldn't make a decision. I didn't want to give Rocky a divorce, but he filed it, and he had also changed to a pretty strong lawyer.

Then September 11th happened, so I was already depressed. I thought Rocky would come back because everybody was so sad at the time of September 11th. I thought he would have a heart and come back to his family. I hoped he would feel the family was most important at a time like that, but he did not come back, or could not. One day I was watching the news, and I saw this girl standing in lower Manhattan holding a sign with her father's picture on it and the words, "Has anyone seen my dad?" The sign popped out at me, and I said to myself, "I can't believe it! My kids have a dad, and he will not come and see his kids. He hasn't seen his kids at all. I know he has been back and forth from Japan, but he didn't come to see his kids. And this girl's father is in the building, already dead maybe, and this girl is looking for her dad. It is not worth it to keep this marriage!"

So I called Leon.

"Leon, I want to give the divorce." Leon said I could file for much more money, because I made much more money than Rocky, but I said, "Leon, I want the restaurant. I want the restaurant building. I want the three kids. The rest, I don't care about anymore. I need my kids because he is not a good father to take care of the kids, and I need the restaurant to support the three kids going to college."

So Rocky got much more than he asked for.

October 10, 2001 was our divorce date. I think it was a Tuesday. It was raining all day long.

Our divorce hearing was scheduled for one o'clock, and I was hoping the hearing would finish by four o'clock, which I thought reasonable, so I could pick Eddie up at five o'clock to drive him to tennis. I told him to wait for me at school, and I took his tennis bag in my car.

The whole time, Rocky would not look at me. He looked away, with a totally evil face, because he got the court reports about our fighting, and I was just numb, stuck in my own head, thinking so many things, but most of all thinking, over and over, "I can't believe I'm getting divorced."

Rocky's attorney had done some paperwork incorrectly, and he wouldn't allow the hearing to continue until he got a chance to amend it. So my one o'clock divorce lasted all the way to almost five minutes to five o'clock, when the court usually closed at the end of the day.

The judge allowed us to reenter the courtroom even though it was pass five o'clock. I was shuffling in, but then I just stopped and started crying. Rocky's attorney came over to hand me a Kleenex, so everyone knew Rocky was the stupid person.

Finally, the judge gave his summarizing statement.

"Mr. Kang, you might think money and friends are very important to you, but when you are getting old, and money is not there for you anymore, when your health is not there anymore, all you have left is the family." The judge said that directly to Rocky, who was standing very close. "Please exercise your right to visit your children, Mr. Kang, and I wish you both the best of luck."

Our divorce was final after that.

Eddie called and said, "Where are you?" It was already past five o'clock. I lied. "I am doing the buying, I don't think I can pick you up. Li is on her way to get you, though."

I hung up the phone and thought about how sad it was to speak to my son moments after divorcing his father, who had become this man who made me suffer so much. I thought, "Look at him. I suffered so much for this man."

After the divorce was final, I walked out into the rain. Leon, my lawyer, gave me a huge, big hug, and said, "Dee, just forget everything and move on." He was really nice. Leon could have charged me much more in the course of negotiating a more complicated divorce that would have gotten me more money, but he understood my concerns when I told him I really didn't care about the rest of it if I could have the kids and the restaurant. I told him, "Leon, I know you are a lawyer. You are supposed to get a lot for your client, but that is not my way. I want to work my way," and he was willing to work my way.

When the divorce was settled, Rocky gave me two months to move out of the house. If I took longer than two months, he informed me, he was going to charge me $330 per day. That was October 10th, so on December 10th, I had to move out of the house.

After my divorce, I was very scared to see everyone, even my own mother. It seemed like while the ordeal was going on, right up until the point it ended, nobody in my family was checking to see how everything was going or anything.

I only made one attempt to update the family during that time. I had shared the story of what was going on at Chinese New Year's Eve in February 2001. That New Year's, we all went to my mom's house, as was our tradition, all my brothers and sisters and everyone who comes along with them. They did feel sorry for me, and they felt scared for me, but nothing of practical worth came out of their mouths, nothing like, "Oh, sister, you should get a divorce!" No, zero stuff like that.

My brother said, "What is going on with you guys? How can you let all the Japanese people come and ask me about it without letting me know? How do you want me to answer them?" I got so sad. This was the brother I helped when he was building a business, and I felt like he was not comforting me.

"Whatever you want to tell them, just tell them. You don't have to ask me." I didn't hear a comforting word from him, and I was kind of disappointed by that, but I didn't have the heart to hate him, because I was so full of everything else.

I started looking for houses in Northbrook and Glenview. When I started looking for houses, I realized that I didn't want to go to Northbrook, especially, because all my nephews and nieces already lived there. However, one of the two houses I ended up liking was there.

I have a friend who is a broker, and she helped me a lot. The first house she found me, the Northbrook house I liked despite the proximity of my family, was sort of new, but there was no basement. I kind of liked the newness, because I am not a handy person.

I said, "If I lived in the older house," which belonged to her friend, and was only thirteen years old, for that matter, "I might have to fix things here and there. But it does have a very nice basement." And I couldn't make the choice.

I called Ling, and said, "I can't make a choice between the two houses. Will you come and look at them?"

So I took her to the first house...

Ling liked both of them, but we decided I should take the older house, the one in Glenview.

She told me she liked feng shui, even though she's Christian. You know what feng shui is, right? Christians are not supposed to care about feng shui, but she kind of followed it. She said, "The problem with the new house is that there's a straight line between the front door and the back door, so your money and good fortune will come in the front and go right out the back. The older house doesn't have that problem." Okay?

"Also, the stairs face the front door right away, which is not good. The stairs are supposed to be hidden on the side." Right.

So the older house had feng shui going for it, but I didn't take it for that. I took it for a basement, because I knew I would need a basement.

I closed on the Glenview house on December 10, but the earliest I could move into my new house was December 28, so for eighteen days I had nowhere to go.

My mom had plenty of room in her four-bedroom house, but I didn't want to go to my mom's house.

She didn't even volunteer for me to come, anyway, so I booked a motel suite at the Hampton Inn. We spent Christmas there, since I had to take the kids out of the house.

Every morning, I would take my kids to school then go pick them up and take them back there. We had the same breakfast every day, first thing in the morning, complimentary muffins and apples.

Everyday, I sat there eating that complimentary breakfast and reading the Bible. I felt like, if I didn't have a Bible, I would just get lost right away. At night, after I put the kids in bed, I would come downstairs and read the Bible in the lobby.

Once I knew Rocky was living in Japan with a girlfriend, there were so many times I wanted to kill myself. There were so many times on the highway—you know how sometimes you're in rush hour traffic sometimes, and there's a truck in front of you, and a truck in back of you? When I was in the middle, there were so many split seconds I wanted to just hit the car in front, and then be hit in the back by the truck behind, and then just go on to death. There were so many moments I wanted to kill myself, to jump someplace else, to simply and abruptly disappear.

I even took a trip to China right after the divorce. I said, "Maybe I can just jump someplace and disappear, totally disappear, because I just can't take the pressure."

And the shame! There was also the shame. I'm from the Chinese community. I couldn't take the whispers I imagined: "They got divorced."

I shared this with my niece. "Li, I really wanted to kill myself today. I just didn't have the guts. Every time I think about doing it, I don't worry about Eddie that much, you know, because I know Eddie is pretty mature. Eddie is pretty independent, you know? I know Mari will be okay. Mia is in the fourth grade now..." Every time I thought of Mia, though, I just couldn't do it. "If I didn't have Mia, I'd probably just kill myself, I'd just smash through that truck, you know? Just a split second, you know, okay?"

Oh my God, after I shared this to my niece, and I knew I HAD to share this with my niece, it caused big trouble. So many times, after my niece finished her work at the restaurant, she would not go home. She escorted ME home, to make sure I didn't try anything, and then she would park outside, at the end of my long driveway, sleeping in the car, waiting to see if I was going to do something stupid. If she was worried, she was ready to come in right away. She did that so many nights, and I didn't know.

In the mornings, she would call me. "Auntie, are you okay?" I'd say, "Yeah, I'm fine, you know, okay?"

Later on, when I got better, she shared the story. She said, "Auntie, I have spent so many nights sleeping on your driveway.

Did you know?" After I heard that, I almost wanted to hit the truck and kill myself once again, out of shame for putting her to such a sacrifice, but I felt I had recovered my mental health, due to her support, enough so that I could express my deepest gratitude for her presence in my life.

"I have to live Li, because I have such people that love me so much. I have the kids near me; I cannot let myself let those people down anymore. You are like an angel to me; you are more than an angel to me. I can't do this anymore, so I have to wake up." I encouraged myself. "I have to wake up."

On Christmas Eve and Christmas Day we get very busy, because my Jewish customers have nowhere to go but to eat Chinese. I needed the money that year, because I was totally bare, so I decided to open both days.

Eddie volunteered to come in and help out at the restaurant. I didn't have a busboy, since they'd fired the last guy, and you can't get a one-day-help busboy.

"Mom, I'm going to come help you this Christmas. Do I need to dress up?" He asked.

"Well, listen now. Change your gym shoes. You've got to have a pair of black shoes." He had a pair, so he wore them and came in to do the busboy job.

The first table he cleaned was also his last. He took the water glasses and everything to the kitchen, and I heard a crashing noise. He kind of slid on the kitchen floor, and a glass broke just as he fell to the floor and cut him right around the eyes. He started to bleed, and at the same time, people were lining up at the door.

My son was bleeding, and I was the only one there to see the customers lined up at the door to their tables.

Mashi wasn't there, because I had let him have the night off, and I didn't know what to do for a moment. I called one of the deliverymen and said, "Take Eddie to Grant Hospital."

My mind was worried about Eddie, and I had customers. It

was crazy busy that night.

After I finished everything, I called Eddie on the cell phone.

"Mom, I just came out. I had four stitches."

"Eddie, stay there. I'll go pick you up, okay?" and I went to the hospital and picked him up.

I took Eddie back to the motel. We didn't say anything. I was just so tired, even crying. Eddie went to bed right away. Thank God he was okay: right up on the eyes there, four stitches. A little bit more and he could have gotten killed there. He could have been blinded.

Li found out, I don't know how. In the middle of the night, she came over and knocked on my door. I went downstairs and held her, crying so bad. I cried so bad.

Every time I got as sad as that, she always had the best of sentiments coming out of her mouth to comfort me.

"Dee, Auntie, it's okay. This is only going to make Eddie strong, so don't worry about it. Even if nobody likes us in this world, God loves us. Things happen for a good reason. Look at it on the bright side: Eddie didn't get blinded," Li said.

So we spent that Christmas at the Hampton Inn. We didn't have a Christmas meal. None of my brothers or sisters offered me a place at their table, and I didn't want to go see my mom.

So moving day came. On the 28th of December, I checked out of the Hampton Inn.

I had a mover coming at 9:00 in the morning to move our stuff to the new house. But when the movers came, I was just numb. I was standing there, numb, when my niece came to help me move.

I didn't have anybody in my family coming but Li, and there was all this, this stuff. I didn't know what to do. None of my kids were home, although they had offered to help. I sent them away because I didn't want them to go through the pain of leaving their home. Just to help me pack their daddy's clothes had been too much for them. We took his winter clothes, whatever belonged to him and packed them in three or four boxes, and it hurt them just to write down "daddy's winter clothes" on each box. I could see their tears then, so I didn't want them helping me when I packed and moved the entire house. I told Mari to go to Winter Break, and Eddie was someplace for a tournament, and Mia was probably visiting a friend. I much preferred to have only myself doing this work.

Before we started, Li said, "Auntie, you know what? When people have to walk down this road, they still have to go one step at a time, they cannot jump or do anything to avoid going through all 10,000 miles. To move out of here is sad, Auntie. You cannot jump or do anything, one step at a time to the truck, and eventually you will be finished."

That's what she told me, and it encouraged me a lot, hearing those words. So we started the move at nine o'clock in the morning, moved to the new house all day, and finished at eleven o'clock at night.

Those movers were so nice; they didn't even take a break. I brought them lunch, and they didn't even sit down to eat. They were moving as they put their lunch in their mouths. Very nice.

I was ensconced at the new house, starting to settle down, and trying to come out of the divorce.

After the New Year, I wanted to encourage myself to come out of the divorce, so I accepted a wedding invitation. I hadn't joined a big Korean-born Chinese event for a long time, going through all my crises. The invitation I accepted came from one of the people I know whose son was getting a second marriage.

At the beginning, I didn't want to go. Then Li said, "Auntie, you should go! I'll watch the restaurant if you will go."

"Okay," I said to myself, "you should, you should go, then." I was kind of encouraging myself. I should go. I should come out of this.

So that day, I felt like it was the only day I looked so pretty in a long time. That day, somehow, I put mascara on, and I looked so pretty. I needed to put on a good face for the wedding.

My friend's son's wedding was held in one of the country clubs. I had never been there, so I got lost, and I was thirty minutes late, which meant I was walking directly into the wedding banquet, having missed the ceremony. It was noisy as I approached, but the whole room totally quieted down when I opened the door. Every face was on me. I can pretend pretty well, so I just made myself feel like nothing was happening, and I went to say hi to these people, hi to that table. It was silent for I don't know how long, then people started to look at me and whisper. I didn't know what they were saying about me, but I knew something was going on. They were talking about me—saying something about me.

I didn't want to feel down in there, because I promised myself I was going to come out of it, so I put a big, huge, face on myself, you know?

After things were finished, my niece's mom asked me, "Dee, can you take me home? Will you volunteer to take me and your auntie home?" My mother's brother's wife was there, too, and she didn't have a car. "Sure, not a problem." I had even danced with everyone, to every song. I don't know how to dance, but you know?

While I was driving, taking them home, my niece's mom started questioning my auntie. "Why did you tell people about Dee?" It was painful, trying to drive with two people sitting in the back having that kind of conversation. "It's already bad, why'd you have to tell them all the details. It's none of their business, okay?" Now I knew why people talked about me. When I wasn't there, and they thought my auntie was family, they were asking her how we divided assets! Yes, and my auntie didn't even know, but she started to tell people how we divided the assets! And all those people discussed the information among themselves, and it got very widespread and really distorted.

One person says, "Oh, yeah..." The next person said, "Blah blah

blah." That's how they started talking the minute I walked into the wedding banquet.

I started crying and said, "Auntie, how can you do this to me? You're supposed to be on my side. You know how hurt I was without your saying anything. You're not even on my side if you have to tell people how Rocky and I divided. Even if he got more, okay, he's my kids' father! He has a right to get more, okay? At least I didn't give that money to the attorney, or give it to other people! I gave it to him! So what is the matter if he got more money, if he doesn't know how to use that money? I didn't get that much, as you know? I didn't get what I was supposed to get. But I can wisely guard my money to make more. You know? So why did you have to tell other people?" I was totally upset.

Then she felt sorry. She said, "Oh, I wasn't trying to cause trouble..."

"Blah, blah, blah!" Somehow it just came out of my mouth. I was totally nuts.

When I got home. I was disappointed in myself. I said, "I sure came out of myself by crying like a crazy woman!"

During the time, Eddie was really starting to mature, seeing everything I was going through.

In our new house, we had one very prominent wall going into the kitchen. After we moved into the new house, and Eddie started a new school, I got so depressed. I would just punch my head into the wall so bad. Over fifty times in a row, POW! POW! POW! I just couldn't take it anymore.

Eddie would get so scared, and Mia as well. After I punched, I cried, and after I cried, it was so bad: I got tired, and I would just fall asleep on the floor, and then Eddie would bring a blanket to cover me.

I was doing this so much that Eddie couldn't take it anymore. He said, "Mom, I'm going to leave this house!"

When Eddie was at New Trier, he was not a great student, but he was a good student. During the divorce, however, he was getting C's, and even some D's, but I couldn't say anything because I knew what he was going through. Somehow, by Christmas, he made it back to B's and A's with only one C, maybe…I can't remember.

Eddie had transferred to Glenbrook South, which had the reputation of being one step below New Trier. When I took him to register, passing the people in the hallway, I saw Polish there, Russian there, Indian there, Black there, and Asian there.

I'm not racist, but as a mom, I started to feel guilty. "My son was going to the best school, and now, because of me, because of my marriage, now he's coming to this school." I felt sorry, okay, so sorry for my son.

So when Eddie actually started attending Glenbrook South, I was so scared to ask him even one question like, "How is the new school?" I felt like I had no right to ask. Worse than that, I had no face to talk to him about it, my own son. He was still very busy trying to catch up, that much was plain. He was busy with schoolwork because he had to catch up with whatever they had already learned in his English class, which used a different book from his English class at New Trier. The English Department at Glenbrook South had at least kind of respected Eddie's New Trier English preparation, because they let him into his new English class right away, without making him take a test.

Mia was so nice by that time. She was well guarded in the Christian school. Every morning, they prayed for Mia, so Mia wasn't even ashamed to share the story, because everybody was praying for her, since they would dedicate a devotion time to sharing the story. But while Mia kind of opened herself and shared, Eddie was not okay.

He totally blew out one day.

Yet, by the time spring break was coming, I felt like I could see happiness on Eddie's face, and then I started catching him smiling. Eddie started making friends. He caught up with the Glenbrook

South English class, which might have been the thing that made him happy; it certainly made me happy, too. I could see it: Eddie was getting better.

One day I would see a black kid bring him home. One day I would see an Asian kid bring him home, which surprised me, because before going to Glenbrook South, Eddie had a certain pride, at New Trier, about holding himself apart—he didn't even talk to Asian kids at New Trier. He wanted nothing to do with them, and he didn't seem like he was Asian himself, because he could compete nationally in tennis. Most of the New Trier parents were doing pretty well, living good, so he thought he was half-Jewish, and he wanted nothing to do with minority activities or anything like that.

When we moved to Glenbrook South, and I started seeing Asian kids bringing him home, and he started to get Asian friends, and he started to get black friends, and he told me he had a Polish friend. I said, "Wow, thank God. My calculation is never near close to your calculation, Lord. Thank you, God, for letting me move to Glenbrook South." Now I know why God wanted us to move to Glenbrook South.

Do you know why? It was to show us, to deliver us into, the diversity of how people live a normal life. North Shore life is not normal, and normal life is not like North Shore life.

I started to feel comfortable myself, and to move on from the emotional intensity of the time our family spent in limbo.

As I continued to come out of my divorce, I still had to deal with the restaurant. I couldn't decide whether to close down or move on from the pain and continue in business. I felt like I had no guts to close down, but I didn't know what to do with the space anymore. It was too old. Everything was old, which caused so many problems. I would fix one part, and then the next part would go on the fritz. I thought, "I just don't know what to do anymore."

Close down or move on! I had been making more money than

$700 but it still wasn't what it used to be.

What it used to be! You kind of compare with what used to be, and it's very hard to humble yourself and say, "This is me." You have to face the fact, you know, you do, but it's hard. One part of me—and suddenly, I had to face this fact—one part of me still made comparisons with the old times. How good they were! Sometimes I came in, and only twenty or thirty people ate at Dee's all night! Before we would be closing the restaurant, and twenty or thirty people would have been turned away, crying that we should stay open!

One day, I woke up and felt like, "I've got to remodel." I knew I had to do something to start over. That question, at least, was settled.

Well, it was settled when I had energy, which was not yet all of the time.

Some days, I would get up and say, "Oh, let's just close the door on the restaurant. Let's just let it go. I can rent out the space, probably, and live on the rent. Let's just forget about it, okay?

I was back and forth, back and forth, from after the divorce all the way until after July 4th.

But that one day, I woke up with a very clear mind telling me, "Dee, this is your baby. You have to take care of your baby, you cannot let your baby go, all right?"

And realizing this, realizing that the restaurant was and is one of my babies, all of the sudden I started calling architects and contractors to manage the challenges of remodeling the business.

We started to work on blueprints in July, August, and September. I told the contractor, "Promise me I can open back up in two months." Our original plan was to close one section at a time, so we could keep the other one open, but as often happens when you're working at the drawing board, as you're drawing, the plans get bigger and bigger and bigger, and finally I had to totally close down the restaurant.

Li said, "Auntie Dee, maybe this is the time you should take a little time off," since we were going to be closed for two months.

I thought about it, and I started making plans to go see my cousin in California, whose wedding I had skipped because I was going through my divorce, although, true to the patterns of behavior in my family, I didn't tell her that was why, choosing, instead, to simply ignore the invitation she so graciously sent me. I wanted to go visit her, and from there drive to Las Vegas, then Arizona, too, for a couple of days rest.

I had all this planned for when the construction was going on, but I didn't go anywhere. From the day I closed, I came to the restaurant every single day. I didn't go anywhere, but I did stay home at night, which felt like a vacation, and my helpers were so nice. I had given them one month off, with a month's pay if they came in and helped me with demolition for one month. One staff member came in and worked on it, and after one month, I gave him a one-month vacation.

But I didn't go anywhere. I was there to watch the workers every single day besides Saturday and Sunday, to push them and encourage them so I could open on time. But the more you go in, the more problems you find, so I spent much, much more money than I was supposed to. Finally, there was no way, with all the problems I found, that I was going to open up, but the head contractor was so nice, he started to volunteer to come in on the weekend to work for me.

Some days, he would just come himself, and some days, Sunday especially, he would bring his son to work for me at his side, and so it was really heart-to-heart. I would buy coffee and donuts, but they seemed so funny about it: they wouldn't drink my coffee, I slowly realized. I didn't know about their company policy. They told me they did some work for this one restaurant, and they were given coffee throughout the job, but then, towards the end, charged for everything they had consumed, so it was their company policy not to avail themselves of such offerings. Okay, I understood.

At one point, I felt there was no way anybody coming to this restaurant-slash-building site would believe it was going to reopen December 1st, but I told them, "Promise me I'm going to open up," and I had become pretty good friends with the owner, Michael, who is really nice, and he came to know what I was going through in my personal life.

I opened the restaurant back up on December 1st, exactly on time.

We had just reopened the restaurant. When a restaurant has already gone down once, it is even harder to accept the reality that I knew well from the early, cash-poor months of the original Dee's: it is very difficult to make it right away. I started coming out to work seven days a week, and I worked really hard, table-to-table. The thing that kept me going, as I tried my best to entice our customers into making Dee's a regular stop on their rounds of Lincoln Park, was looking around and thinking to myself, "At least the restaurant is brand new." Depression was still there—I could feel it lurking—but less and less, because I was too tired to get depressed, too busy to think about it. Also, as the real saving grace, I still had my wonderful niece helping me.

Living in a new suburb, my daily routine involved a lot of driving back and forth on the highway. I had to ask Eddie to be the father and mother for Mia every night, since the best I could do was skip out on the late-afternoon prep work for a speedy drive to pick her up at private school, drop her off at home, and get back to work in time for the dinner rush. Mari was almost grown, but I didn't call her. Once in a while, she came home, but there was no connection or anything. I never sent her a package or anything, and I'll say it again, because I don't think I can stress it enough: I never called her or anything. I was pretty much focused on the restaurant.

It was hard not having the right amount of business in the dining room. Sometimes, you're standing around, when it's really so, so slow, and you start to wonder, "Are the other places slow, too, or is it just my place? Should I start checking around?" Well, let me tell you, you feel not-so-bad, if not exactly better, when the places you check are slow, too, but when you learn for a fact that other places are busy and yours is slow, it hurts a lot. Finally, after I'd been doing that for a short period of time, I told myself, "You know what? This is not right. You cannot compare the business now with what it used to do."

"What is more," I realized, in an upwelling of competitive spirit that thankfully blocked off the entirely opposite response of considering giving up from even entering my mind, "I cannot let the business down."

It's just excessive, just too much to close down when you run into problems. You can't put yourself through that unless it is really time for you to do something else with your life.

You can't compare yourself with what the business used to do before. You have to tell yourself, "This is the beginning. This is what I just started with. If I don't have any expectations, if I don't use the past as a benchmark, and I make some money, then I'm making money, and a positive trend has begun." I started thinking things like that to myself a lot, and from that point, I didn't go and see what other restaurants were doing anymore. "They can be packed, with people waiting at the door," I told myself. "It's okay."

"Whatever comes into my door, this is my business. These are customers who came to me, so I'll take good care of them." Once you give yourself that statement, you are free. Otherwise, it's really painful to check around the competition. It's not a good feeling to do that. It's not a good feeling.

Actually, I was pretty happy for that revelation, which allowed me to have patience as I rebuilt the dining-in component of my business.

The carryout and delivery side of the business has always done very well, but I made a big mistake, during this reconstruction period, to put in a brand-new computer system. I had worked with this company for over ten years. Around the time I was resurrecting Dee's, they had just come out with a new system. The father and son who run the company came and demonstrated it for me, and I thought I could trust their technology, because I used the old one for over ten years with good results.

I put the new system in, and, oh my God, I was the tester. When you redo, you want to be at least 100 percent sure the system is working, but we were like the first or second ones to try out the system. One problem after another problem for two months, continuing every single day; the problem that made me the angriest was when the tickets that were supposed to come out of the machine in the kitchen disappeared, or at least wouldn't come out. I had so many delivery orders that the kitchen never knew about. It was a nightmare the first three months. One time we even had some other restaurants receive the printouts for our restaurant. Then the funny thing was bills that would be, say, $40, which were supposed to have a delivery charge of $2.50 added, would stubbornly cap the total customer invoice at $40, even though the $2.50 was right there, as if the machine refused to add up to the real total of $42.50. The delivery charge was right there, but the machine wouldn't add it in, so I told the computer company, "You have to pay me for that." Thank God my deliverers found out about the calculating error, because half the tickets would come back to me edited by hand, and it's not that I wanted to make money at the company's expense, but I wanted them to pay me because even the $20 a day it was costing me was a lot in the beginning days of the new Dee's.

Chinese people don't have a good return system. I think American people, something they don't like, even something they wear once, they return. But for us...we're not returning people. We didn't grow up thinking we can just return something we don't like, so we don't even like returning what has to be returned. Don't think I haven't considered the irony of this attitude in personal relationships.

I introduced my computer company to one of my neighbor restaurants, and they had the same problem as ours, but they returned the computer system right away. Because I had over ten-some years' connection with this company, I had such problems with my computers for a long time. I have to say this: whenever you close down to reopen a restaurant, you have to make sure every department is right. I had a huge ticket problem, hugely, for two months.

Anyway, the carryout business was doing well, but the dining was slow. My customers came in just to see me, and many people clearly liked the feeling of telling me they were glad I came back to work, but with my family still in crisis, I kept thinking of something which they could not really have been aware of: they were happy to see me, but I was there at work every single day, which meant that every single day, Mia and Eddie had to struggle without Mom.

It was very hard. Every time I managed to pick Mia and Eddie up and bring them home, and get everything for dinner on the table, 5:00 p.m. approached, and I had to start getting ready to come out of the house for my dinnertime shift at work. In winter, there was not so much visibly going on in the neighborhood to remind me of the family time I had to miss, but in the summertime, I saw mom and dad and the kids playing basketball outside on their driveway, or riding bikes together, precisely at the time I had to totally rush up my commute, trying not to get stuck in traffic, and inevitably, blamelessly failing, on my way to the restaurant.

It was really guilty-feeling to barely situate and then virtually abandon the kids every single day. At least on Fridays, I took Mia to youth group at church, which made me feel less bad because she wasn't cooped up at home, but otherwise, six days a week, I had this guilt. Then again, if I stayed home, I worried about the restaurant, so I went back and forth, back and forth, always carrying this guilt inside.

By the summer, the restaurant was doing okay. There was no comparison with the sales I was used to making, but it was okay, and also so new, and so clean—everything was so clean—that I started to really find the joy in being there in the summertime.

In June 2003, when we had been reopened not even one year, six months, really, since we reopened December 1, 2002, I was working at the new Dee's on a Wednesday night. The next day would be my birthday. Emily was answering the phone. I noticed the phone ringing—nothing exceptional—and saw her talking—nothing unusual. Then she said, "Dee, I think you should be the one to answer this call."

The Sadness Flowed Like Wine

"They're looking for Rocky. I know we usually just say he's no longer here, but they're calling from Japan speaking full English," she said. So I picked up.

A man's voice told me he was Mr. blah, blah, blah, calling from the American Consulate in Osaka, Japan, looking for somebody who knew Robert Kang. I said, "I am his ex-wife," and he told me he had to give me bad news. At that moment, right away, I knew something had happened to Rocky, and then Mr. blah, blah, blah told me he had had an accident, although later that was revealed to be a half-true story he was merely telling me for the moment.

Mr. blah, blah, blah spoke some English words I didn't totally understand, but now I realize he told me Rocky had a head injury, in the front, and they had to operate on him to take the blood out to relieve pressure on his brain. The man told me Rocky was still unconscious in the hospital, and he gave me all the information about this hospital, and then he said, "You probably want to call them and ask them more about it. Because Mr. Kang is a U.S. citizen, they notified us at the Embassy right away."

I called the hospital phone number and said, in Japanese, "I am Dee Kang, I received a call from the American Consulate, and I would like to find out more information about my ex-husband, Robert Kang." She would not release any information, however, because I was not legally with him anymore. Finally, I said, "My daughter is twenty-one, but she doesn't speak fluent Japanese. Can you release this information to me so I can tell his daughter?" They still would not do that, but I was very fortunate that night to have a regular customer who is part of the Chamber of Commerce in Osaka sitting at the sushi bar. He was in Chicago for a conference, and he asked me what had happened when I hung up the phone after being rebuffed. I told him, and he said, "Well, let me make a phone call for you." He took the number, and he called and said, "I have a right to ask you for information about this man's condition, I am working for blah, blah, blah..." Finally, my Japanese customer found out all the information. To begin with, they told him, Rocky had been hurt in a fight, not an accident per se. He told me that they said Rocky was still unconscious from his injuries, even though they had performed the surgery successfully.

When I found out about the fight, I realized that Mashi already knew. He didn't tell me because he didn't want me to get involved with Rocky again.

They also told him that Rocky only had a 5 percent chance to live.

The kids started to cry when I told them, and after reassuring them that everything would be all right and we were going to see about their dad, I didn't wait at all to order our tickets. We spent my birthday packing and preparing, and took a flight to Japan on Friday, June 27, 2003.

But as I laid awake during the thirteen-hour flight, I questioned myself "why?" While I felt that I did not have an answer, God answered me. He told me I must get Robert. Defiantly, I thought to myself and said to God, "I don't want to bring Robert back." Again I asked, "Why should I?" Once again God replied, "Because you must." Reluctantly, and with a very, heavy heart, I agreed.

When I arrived in Japan, it was night, and we couldn't go to the hospital right away for two reasons. One, Rocky's girlfriend was there. Two, intensive care in Japan is very strict. Visiting is two hours during the day and two hours at night. You cannot pass beyond those windows of time by even one minute. Japanese people all have internalized this very strict concept of time, so they don't go over almost by nature. We, the kids and I, decided to wait until morning, and then I got a hold of Rocky's cousin, who offered us a place to stay.

In the morning, when we arrived at Intensive Care during visiting hours, we all had to put on a special gown. We went inside, and stayed for as long as we could. The kids hadn't seen Rocky for over two years, so to see him lying on the bed, our tears just came out. We cried to see his head, so swollen they had to take the scalp off in one place to get at a bone in his skull, which they had to cut in half, lengthwise, to give the swelling a little more room. Rocky's head was still swelling when we finally arrived there. He looked so scary, and there was still blood everywhere.

Rocky was in a coma, with an audience of the same three friends he was with the night he hit his head, including the one who got in the fight with him. The doctor said they had been coming there every single day, 12:00 until 2:00 p.m. Only three people could go in at a time, so I let the kids spend the whole two hours in there while I stood outside and talked with these men.

I found out they had all gotten drunk together for the first time in a while that night, because one man, who owed Rocky money, had disappeared for a long time before showing up to go out to dinner out of the blue. After dinner, they got into an argument, and then went to another place for drinks, where the argument only got louder. Rocky and the friend who owed him money were the first to burst out of the sushi bar, where they started throwing punches in the street.

The other friend came out and saw Rocky punching the man who owed money really bad, so he started punching Rocky, but they were so drunk that just one punch knocked Rocky out. They said he hit the concrete curb with the back of his head, and passed out cold.

Rocky's friends thought he was just drunk, drunk enough that he couldn't, or wouldn't, get up, but in no serious danger, so they waited there for thirty minutes. Rocky still wouldn't get up, so they asked for some cold water from the sushi bar. They poured it all on Rocky. But even after it was all gone, Rocky still wasn't waking up. At that point, they noticed it was serious, and only then did they call the ambulance.

At the time of his injury, it appeared to hospital staff that Rocky might regain full consciousness in a matter of hours. They did a CT scan right away, and though they saw bleeding in the front brain, it was just a little bit, not obviously as serious as the hit in the back. Rocky seemed to be awakening as they settled him in for close observation, but the next morning his breathing had totally degraded in quality and strength. They did an emergency surgery on him right away.

They took some tissue samples from his brain, and it was so swollen, the doctor said, that they had to cut the scalp out to give the pressure a little bit of release, and the doctor said that was as far as they'd gotten before I arrived. It was all right now, the doctor said. Rocky was in stable condition.

But I had to sit down with the doctor and ask what the condition would become, for the sake of our children, who had traveled so far to be with their dad, so the doctor gave me all the information he had. The doctor said, "With head injuries, everybody's different. Chances are, Robert will live, but we don't know how well he will function. His brain function may be from 40 to 80 percent of his former capability. It will never be 100 percent. The highest will be 80 percent, the lowest 40 percent, but within that range, we don't know if he's going to walk or not, because he's still not waking up at this time. There are a lot of things doctors don't know, okay? And that's all we know."

Everyday, we went to the hospital from 12:00 to 2:00 p.m.

My kids insisted, because there seemed to be so many small ways in which Rocky needed their care. There was still a lot of blood behind his ears, so Mia was asking for hot towels, wiping it off for her dad. Eddie had a tennis ball with him, so Eddie kept giving his dad a treatment where he put the ball in Rocky's hands and told him to squeeze, trying to hold Rocky's hand to make him squeeze when he didn't respond. I guess Rocky never took care of himself, because his hands were really so dry, and the nails were so long. I asked for a nail cutter to cut his nails for him, but the skin was too dry, so I asked the nurse for some oil and started rubbing it in. The kids really loved him so much, and every day, we just cried and cried and cried...

Rocky's girlfriend went at night, from 5:00 to 7:00 p.m. Rocky's friends told me his girlfriend wanted to sit down with me, and I thought I had to sit down with her.

Because I left so rushed, I didn't have time to pack. I had to take care of the restaurant's bills and everything before I left, and I think I took the 8:00 a.m. flight from Chicago to Detroit, then changed to a Northwest Airlines flight to Japan, so I didn't sleep all night as I worked on the paperwork. All I had was three t-shirts, three sets of underwear, and three pairs of pants. That's all I packed for Japan! And I wore size 1X, Japan doesn't have a 1X size.

It was so hot when we arrived, I felt like I was sitting in a sauna. The next day, traveling between the hospital and the hotel we found after the first night, I was miserable from the humidity. I told the kids, "I used to live in Osaka, but I never knew it was this hot. Maybe I was young, you know?" I sweated, and my t-shirt got wet, and in an air-conditioned space, it would dry, and then get wet with sweat again when I went out into the heat. I hated that I could see the sweat, but I didn't have anything to change into. Japan, unlike here, is not well provisioned with coin-operated washing machines for the use of the public, and I hated the thought of going to Rocky's cousin's house to do laundry.

So the day I was to sit down with Rocky's girlfriend, I looked so miserable.

When I walked into the coffee shop area, I saw her. She was sitting at a table with a Prada bag, Ferragamo shoes, some designer jeans, and a Chanel t-shirt. I was wearing uncomfortable, soiled travel clothes. I looked at her outfit and said to myself, "That's all the money...I work hard, and she has all that on her. You think she earned that? No, Rocky bought it for her!"

I looked at myself, and I felt like crying more. But I shut off my tears as best I could and tried to give the impression of being very strong, which is actually how I felt the more I thought about how I had mostly earned the money my husband had given her.

"Mrs. Kang, I don't know how to show my respect for you," she said.

"Well, I guess we have to be brave and come up with a direct answer: what are you going to do? Are you going to be taking long-term care of him? You realize the doctor says he's going to be anywhere from 40 to 80 percent. I hope it's 80, but if it's 40 percent, do you have the heart to take care of him?"

"No," she said. "I can only take care of him right now, okay? I can't make a long-term commitment. I am still young."

"Okay," I said, "How old are you?" That's when she told me she was thirty-five years old, and then she asked me what I was going to do.

"If you're not going to...I give you first choice, because you're with him right now, but if you're not going to take care of him, I'm going to take him back to America."

She never asked a question about me. At that point, I didn't know how hard it was going to be to take care of Rocky. I had no knowledge, nor did I have the experience to take care of him, but that's what I said.

I wasn't sure how exactly I would do that if he didn't regain consciousness.

"I'm going to get the private jet or something, and I'll fly him back," I told her.

"That's fine. I'm going to bring Rocky's stuff to the hotel here. You call me if you need anything, okay?"

The next day, I got five boxes of Rocky's stuff. She just came in and left it in the lobby. The kids and I had to bring his stuff to our room. We sorted it out, taking some stuff, leaving the rest. She didn't come in to see what we kept. I thought, "Well, that's it." She was still going to see him in the ICU, but I felt I had some serious preparations to make when I went back to America.

Eddie had a tournament around the week of August, so we had to go back home. Mia was also homesick, so I left Mari in Japan. She stayed with Rocky's cousin and could easily go see him every day.

Rocky started to regain consciousness, so Mari began calling me every day, giving me reports. In the beginning, he would wake-up, open his eyes a little bit, and go back to sleep. Then Mari started to realize that her daddy was starting to recognize her, and she started to recognize her daddy, because Rocky started to swear a lot, and started wanting to eat a lot of cookies. Mari bought him little cookie packages from the hospital vending machines, and Rocky would eat them all.

Then we found out Rocky could walk. He still slipped a lot, so Mari helped him with it every day.

Though I wanted to bring Rocky back to America right away, the doctor said, "Let's wait, it's not a good idea, because the head injury is still pretty bad." But Mari had to come back soon, because school started in August. Eddie went there after the tournament to take Mari's place because I didn't trust his friends.

When Eddie went there, Rocky started becoming conscious a lot. He started to talk a little more. I even talked to him over the phone once. Eddie said Rocky was not slipping as much when he tried to get up. And Rocky knew Eddie, and remembered Eddie, more and more. One day Eddie told me Rocky had to go through another surgery, because the doctors needed to clean an infected bone and put it back in the skull. They also started to take some of Rocky's tubes out. So, step, step, step, he started to come back.

Finally, Eddie called me and said, "Mom, the doctor said daddy can get out of the hospital by August 30th or 31st."

Before the doctor released him, he warned me. "I don't know why you have to do this. I understand you are divorced from him. It's not easy to take care of him, because of the spot he injured. He will either be good or bad at various times. There's no middle."

The doctor put an example to me. "He will be very rude. For example, if somebody's very fat, okay? We don't say to people directly, 'You're so fat!' But Robert doesn't care. He will just say to your face, 'you're very fat! You're ugly!' Do you understand? He has no flexibility about what to say and what not to say or do."

I really didn't think about how bad it could be, even though the doctor kept trying to warn me. Still, I ordered two business class tickets and went back to Japan for Rocky's release from the hospital. The day before Labor Day, which was a Sunday, we came back to America.

To make it through the trip, the doctor gave him two sleeping pills to make sure he wouldn't wander during the flight, so he was really good. I got on the flight, gave him two sleeping pills, and we came back. He slept the whole time, thirteen hours.

Rocky finally took a bathroom break when we arrived in Detroit. He was so skinny, so weak. I had to hold him all the way. I had to hold him everywhere he went. I did not know it at the time, but he could not see.

We made it back, and he didn't ask the questions I had been warned to expect and prepare for like, "Whose house is this?" He just looked like he had been living there the whole time. The next day, at nighttime, I let him sleep in the nicer bedroom.

But he didn't remember Mia at first. She was at home with him and Rocky said, "Why is there always this woman around, this young lady living in our house?"

"That's Mia, that's your daughter," I said.

"No, I have a daughter named Mia, but Mia is not that big. You didn't fool around with some other man, have a baby, and then think you could trick me into raising her, did you? My Mia is this big. They might have the same name, but that's not Mia!"

Then I thought about it. He may be right—sincere, that is, because he left when Mia was that big, so after whatever, two years, she probably does look way bigger. Mia's the one who grew the most from eight to ten years old. Eddie and Mari didn't change that much in the time Rocky was gone, because Eddie was fourteen, pretty much set. That's why he knew Eddie and Mari.

"Mia, call your dad!" I knew he would recognize her if she spoke to him, that he would recognize her voice and put it together, which he did after a time.

At night, he didn't sleep very much. He would sleep for thirty minutes then wake up then fall back asleep. Again he would wake-up after thirty minutes then sleep. He would wander a lot, too, which was scary. That's how we found out he could not see out of one of his eyes. Even his seeing eye was not right, but he had lost sight altogether in one eye. Everywhere he went I had to hold his hand. I thought, "My God, how am I going to do it? I can't watch him every time he wakes up." But of course that's just what I did. Every time he woke up, I woke up. I didn't want him to fall on his head and hurt it again. That was so hard for me; I couldn't sleep.

My natural instinct was to take care of Rocky myself. I didn't think to hire a nurse, not right away. I just never thought about that. Without any knowledge, without knowing what I was going to do or how to take care of him, I thought: "He can help me if he can walk. It will be good. It will at least be okay."

So Rocky getting better through rehab was my first hope. I

started taking him after we came back. In the beginning, we talked about how to "Rocky-proof" my house. Sofa boxes were placed around the steps, leaving a tiny opening only big enough for a smaller, less clumsy, sighted woman to slide through, so he couldn't pass through to the danger, and a gate was made so that he would not fall down the basement stairs, either.

We went to rehab faithfully, and I wanted to feel it was going to help him, but I started to think, "I guess it's not, because his arms can move okay, his legs can move okay, but his memory, it's like rubber." Twenty years ago, three years ago, everything was all mixed up. I began to say to myself, "The rehab is not working."

He also had to get his eyes examined. When you go see an eye doctor, they have to dilate your eyes. That takes thirty minutes, and Rocky had no patience to wait for anything.

I took him to see the eye doctor, and they dilated his eye. He had to wait thirty minutes. He couldn't wait. He wanted to leave. I said, "Rocky, just a little bit more." I had such a hard time.

Like a little baby, I had to tell him to stay put and say, "I'll buy you coffee; I'll buy you donuts if you do." He even swore at Dr. Gil, and I had to say, "I'm so sorry, he had a head injury, and he just got brain-damaged." The doctor said, "It's okay, don't worry about it."

When I took Rocky down to the lobby, I got so mad. "Rocky, why did you swear at the doctor? This is the doctor who will maybe make your eyesight better, why did you swear?" Rocky looked in my face and said, "I hate you. I hate you for all my life."

Then he looked me in the eye, and spat in my face. We were in the lobby, so there were a lot of other people around. I got so mad and said: "I know where I have to take you now. You don't belong in the house. I have to take you to the mental hospital, because you're crazy. And I am crazy to take care of you."

"You are so funny," he said. "Yes, let's go to the mental home, okay? When we get there, it's not me getting in," he said. "YOU'RE the one getting in. YOU have a problem."

Of course, I knew I didn't have the guts to take him. I didn't even know where it is. So I went home and put an ad in the newspaper for help, because I just didn't think I could do this every single day.

Luckily, I hired a very nice Cantonese lady. She stayed with me. She herself had gotten divorced, and her husband was kind of violent, so she stayed with me, living in the basement, so when I left the house, at least I knew someone was home with Rocky.

Yes, Rocky would swear and fight a lot with her, too.

When he wanted to eat, he could not wait for one minute. If I tended to close a little bit late, he would hunch over the kitchen table like a little child. One time, he told me he didn't want to stay home with the babysitter. He said, in that childish way, "The babysitter smells bad. I don't want to stay with the babysitter. I will swear at the babysitter."

One time, Rocky told me to drive him to this noodle place on Clark Street.

"No, there's no noodle place. I don't think so," I said.

"Yeah, you haven't been there, but there's a noodle place."

So I started to drive him to this noodle place on Clark Street.

"You drive on Clark Street, I'll tell you where to turn."

I drove to Clark on Fullerton, and when I got off Fullerton, I said, "Rocky, where's this noodle place?"

He casually responded, "You go to the corner, and then there's this..."

"Rocky, this is not Osaka, this is Chicago."

"Don't try to talk back to me, just drive. When you get to the corner, you'll see the street name."

All the streets he named were Japanese streets, okay, so he was confused. I stopped the car.

"Do you want me to punch you?" he said.

"Okay, I'll drive." I drove four hours that time, left, right, left, right, looking for his nonexistent noodle shop, so afraid he would hit me. After four hours, Rocky finally got so hungry.

"Rocky, should I go straight? You want to go straight? Let's go there..." I just totally went nuts.

"If you want a hotdog, we'll turn around. There's a hotdog stand over there, okay?" In the end, we ate a hotdog.

Sometimes he would be asleep, and then, in the middle of the night, when he woke up, he would come to my room and want to have disturbing conversations. Sometimes, he wanted to talk about how to kill people. He asked me, "Have you seen the video of how to take the skin off a woman?" I said, "No, I did not." He said, "Oh, I watched this video on how to take the skin out of a woman, and then after that it showed how they killed the woman." I got so scared, and then if I didn't listen to him, he would punch me.

On those nights, when Rocky was sharing how he watched this video about killing a woman, I really got scared, and also, during the day, when I didn't follow his orders, he wanted to punch me. He would say, "You want me to punch you. Come on, you want me to punch you!" and I got scared, because the memory of what he did before would always come back to me.

I felt really endangered, so I put a lock on my master bedroom to keep him away when he got up and wanted to give his horrible midnight talks. In the beginning, when he found a lot of doors not open, he just nicely went back to sleep. One night, however, he found my door was locked, and he pushed and pulled the door off its hinges and the lock out of the wall.

All the knives in my house were hidden and all the scissors.

Frightened, I shared the story with my sister and my mom and some close friends, and they said, "Dee, this is pretty scary, you know? I don't think it's a good idea to be around him." But I just didn't have the guts to take him and put him in some place.

Rocky's memory kept creating problems for him and everybody else. When I went to the restaurant, sometimes I had to bring him there with me. He would sleep in the car, and when I stopped at the red lights, he would say, "Why you stop? You're stupid. You go! If you don't go, somebody is going to chase you and kill you, you know?" He would say it repeatedly, impatiently: "you go, you drive, you go." He had no patience.

If he came into the restaurant, I had to worry about him swearing at the customers, yet there was no way I was going to leave him alone with the babysitter because I was scared Rocky might attack her now that his violence had returned.

So at the restaurant, I either had Rocky sleeping out of sight or with me. But one day, he started to seat customers, bringing them to their tables. Little things like that surprised me a lot. When some customers came in, he knew their names. I said, "Okay, he can seat people." Then I said, "Oh my God, he has no patience!" I saw him swear at customers because they wouldn't follow him right away. When he said, "Table for two, follow me, please," and a customer was still talking, going slowly, he would bend the menu on the table or chair. "You coming or not?" I would have to go and apologize to so many customers. Sometimes, customers would throw a party for eight people, and when they came in, they would stand around saying "hi" to each other, and Rocky would already have the menus on the table, ready to seat them all. When they didn't follow him right away, he would bend the chair. "You coming or not?" He would also swear. Once again, I had to go apologize to customers. "I am so sorry, he had a head injury."

"Oh, okay," they would say.

Another time, at the restaurant, I just couldn't take it anymore. I had to take care of the customers, put on the smiling face for the customers then always deal with the fact that my mind was largely taken up with watching what he was going to do. Finally, one day, I said something, or he did something, I guess, and I got so angry, I called Eddie.

"Eddie, come over here and take your daddy home, I just can't take it anymore, okay? Mom is just so tired. Mom is just so, so tired. Come here and take your daddy home."

Mari was still in school in Champaign.

So he came and took Rocky home. Eddie was so nice. He tried to take care of Rocky one Saturday, even though I really didn't ask Eddie to make that attempt. Eddie complained a little bit about Rocky's behavior, but he tried his best to take care of him.

When Eddie came to the restaurant to take Rocky home, Rocky said something as they reached the car, and Eddie complained or something. Maybe Eddie said, "Why do you have to be this way?" or something, or "If you had never left us, you would never have had all this stuff happen like this." I don't know the composition. Rocky punched Eddie, and Eddie just totally went nuts.

Eddie didn't respond to his dad punching him by jumping in the car and speeding away home, however. Eddie turned around and came into the restaurant. He said, in front of all these people, "Mom, you're crazy, he's not normal!"

I realized Rocky had punched him, because I could see Eddie's face was very red. I had to hold Eddie, take him to the kitchen, and say, "Eddie, I'm sorry."

Then Rocky followed us into the kitchen and said, "You want me to punch you again?" That made Eddie angry.

Eddie said, "You motherfucker! I'm going to kill you!" Then he started to make good on his threat!

There was something on the kitchen counter, and Eddie tried to use it to kill Rocky, and Rocky tried to punch him, so I held Eddie and some other people held Rocky.

Finally, I took Eddie from the kitchen and into the dining room. I marched him from the front to the double doors by the sushi bar, and outside to the car. I opened the passenger side and got in the driver's seat, and drove to a parking lot a little farther away. We were both crying and holding each other, my son and I, both crying so bad, and there was nothing we could say. Eddie was crying like a little baby. I was crying like a little baby.

Then Eddie said, "Mom, he doesn't belong to the family like a normal person, okay? I know you want to, but we can't do this."

After we cried it out, we calmed down. I drove back to the restaurant, picked up Rocky, and drove everybody home.

Eddie tried to take care of Rocky again, so I could get the house all squared away. Rocky liked to go to the Japanese market, so Eddie decided to take his dad and sister there. In the car, I think Rocky said something mean to Mia, who was sitting right behind Eddie, and Eddie took issue, and Rocky punched him again. Mia got so scared, she started crying, and they didn't make it to the market. I sensed something was wrong because they came home so quick, and Mia came to me and said, "Daddy just punched Eddie!" I called out "EDDIE?!" Because I thought Eddie was going to try to kill his dad again.

"Eddie, what happened?"

"Mom, it's my fault. I shouldn't fight with him, it's just he was being mean to Mia, but it's okay." It felt less out of control than the fight at the restaurant, so it was okay, but I could see tears in Eddie's eyes and hear them in his voice. There were so many days like that.

At the same time, I started to see some improvements in Rocky's condition, and in my own ability to get along a little better with him. Like, over time, he started to talk in the car more and more. Right after he came back, he probably slept 80 percent of the time we were in the car. Now he slept half of the time and talked half of the time.

One time, he said, "You remember the hamburgers after we finished playing golf in Hawaii? Those hamburgers were so good, weren't they? I want to have that hamburger again."

"It's not me. I don't play golf. I don't eat hamburger, or at least not those hamburgers. I never played golf with you, it's not me."

It was his girlfriend.

I would kid him by saying exactly that to him, "That's not me, it's your girlfriend." He got so mad. He said, "You always trying to say something bad about me, blah blah blah." Then I got so scared when I was driving him, I had to put my bag in the middle. Then, later on, I got this little voice telling me, "Don't fight with him, have a little...be flexible a little bit."

The next time he said that, it hurt a lot, because I knew it wasn't me, it was his girlfriend who enjoyed that with him, but I said, "Yeah, Rocky, I remember that."

He would repeat the story over and over again. "Yeah, Rocky, I remember the hamburger, that was really good. When you get a little better, we'll go back there. We're going to eat the hamburger again, okay? Yeah. You get better soon, okay?" That made him so happy, just to hear me say that, so I figured I had learned a new technique to take care of him.

He would also say, "Do you know my ex-wife? Gosh, she's such a hard-working woman. But she's too hardworking. She never knew how to enjoy herself."

"Oh, is that right?" I'd say. "Where is she right now?"

"She's living in my house in America."

"Did you give her enough money to live?"

"Yeah, she has the restaurant. You know?"

The entire time, I was sitting right next to him, so you could tell he was drifting in his memories.

Some things he said, I had to ask him, "Rocky, is that recently, or is it twenty-some years ago?" If it was twenty-some years ago, it was a memory of me.

"Do you remember the movie we saw when we first met?" he asked one day.

"How long ago, Rocky?"

"This is a twenty-some-years-ago-story. Do you remember when we first met, I took you to see a movie?"

I really forgot which movies I was seeing at that time.

"You remember, we went to see the boxer Ali movie," he said.

"That's right, yeah."

He remembers these things, I don't. He really remembered a lot of things like that. Everyday I noticed something new.

The first thing I saw was that he liked to go to McDonald's in the morning. One morning, I took him to McDonald's. I let him eat his McDonald's while I put gasoline in the car or bought something small from the store. Usually, when we came back from McDonald's, he'd come and open my door right away.

That day it was supposed to be nice weather, but it was really cold. He came to my side of the car, and he tried to take something out of his pocket. I realized he had bought a coffee for me. He took it out of his pocket.

"I didn't want this coffee to get cold. I was waiting for you, so I put it in my pocket to warm it up for you."

In moments like that, I saw the old softness in him. Just for a second, it would come out. I saw the soft part of him coming out.

Finally, it was time for Rocky to have eye surgery. I made an appointment. The doctor said he had dried blood blocking the vision in the back of his eye sockets, so if we took the blood out, it might improve. The chance of improvement was 50/50, but the doctor said, "If you don't do the surgery, you don't have a chance. If you do, you have a 50 percent chance," so I decided to let him do it.

The doctor said he could not eat after 10:00 p.m. the night before his eye surgery, but Rocky had been eating all day. All night, I didn't sleep, because I wanted to make sure he didn't eat. Every time he woke up, I said, "Rocky, you can't even drink anything." He would swear at me and go back to bed. I didn't sleep at all that night.

I took him to the hospital, and he had eye surgery. The second day after the surgery, I took him to see the doctor, who said, "He can see." That was good, you know, but I was just so tired from everything.

If you could have seen my face, it would have looked so tired. I was so stressed out, but I still saw hope down the road, because Li encouraged me every single day.

"God's blessing is here," she told me. "We don't know the blessings in store, but he will get better." Sometimes, she bought coffee and donuts and brought them to me at home, because she knew I couldn't go out anymore, and she would encourage me, and pray with me. It was so difficult taking care of Rocky, it was non-stop, and Li encouraged me. I saw a little hope, especially for Rocky getting better for some things, if not everything.

When he could remember some very difficult things, I was just so happy. "Oh God, he is improving! Sometimes," I thought to myself, "I misjudge him. He's getting pretty good at some things."

But he still had no patience. I, on the other hand, learned a lot about how to be patient, rather than going directly to struggling or fighting with him. For example, let's say I took him to buy something. I liked to go to the bank, and sometimes I had to take Rocky with me. I learned to ask Rocky to help me. It's not that I really needed his help, of course, but I tried to keep him occupied and moving along in some kind of flow. Sometimes, at the store, he would pick up something and pull it onto the cart, and scatter things all over, and I could see other people thinking, "Crazy man!" But I simply had to take care of things, putting them back patiently, because if I swore at him there in the middle of the store, I was afraid he would punch me, and that would be it: he would be arrested. I tried not to fight with him, even when it was hard for me.

I could tell he was improving every few months. In the first six months, he was really improving a lot. After a year, I could still see the improvement a little bit—even right now, I can still see a little bit of improvement—but it got very slow, very little. Early on though, wow, you could see the change. Rocky started to talk to the kids a lot, too.

About a year after the accident, I decided we should take a family trip to Hawaii. On the flight there, Rocky truly had no patience. All night long, he wandered. I brought the kids, and it was like babysitting for me. I got so tired going there. When we arrived, I said, "Kids, can you please take your daddy out?"

They went out together on the bus, Rocky, Eddie, and Mia, and Rocky changed. He started talking a lot, talking with the kids and making funny faces, making the kids laugh. He just started to have patience.

On that trip, if I said something like, "Rocky, let me take a shower, and we'll go out, okay?" He would wait for me. Before, even if I went to the bathroom, I didn't have time to wash my hands, because he'd be outside the door, knocking, punching the door. In Hawaii, I started to see he had a little patience.

Eddie and Mia took him for an hour, and came back, and then, all of a sudden, Rocky started to dance like John Travolta. I said, "Oh, my God, this is good. This is really good."

On the flight home, I didn't give him a sleeping pill, because I wanted to see how he would do.

He got up; he sat down. The stewardesses told him to sit down, and he didn't swear. You know, he would just sit down! He managed an eight-and-a-half hour flight from Hawaii to Chicago. From that time, Rocky really started to improve a lot.

Though I hadn't played tennis for a long time, I decided I needed to go out to play. I saw this Korean tennis coach I used to know from another club and this little voice said, "Tell Rocky to take a tennis lesson." I also had to say to myself, about the Korean tennis people I knew, "They all know I divorced Rocky."

The tennis instructor also knew Eddie, so I spoke to him very honestly about Rocky and asked, "Do you think that he can try to take a tennis lesson?" He said, "Yeah, we can try."

Rocky took a tennis lesson, and he was able to hit the balls. He still could not see totally clear, not as clear as before the accident, certainly, but his vision was definitely a little better than before the surgery.

When he was hitting the ball, he said "Fuck you, fuck you!" to the tennis balls the whole time. I said, "Coach, I'm sorry, it's the injury. His behavior is either bad or good, and so is everything in the world, to him, everything he tries." The coach said, "Don't worry about it."

Tennis was healthy for Rocky. Rocky had gained so much weight in the process of recovery. He liked to eat some unhealthy things. He liked heavy seasonings, not healthy vegetables.

Tennis helped him improve his diet, because he didn't seem as hungry when he was playing frequently. In the beginning, he took one day a week, for one hour, for tennis. One day turned to two days, and two days turned to three days a week of tennis. Today, he's been playing tennis three days a week for a long time, and I can see he's still improving.

But still, it was very difficult to take care of him. We still had accidents, tons of times.

Once Rocky and Eddie were at home. I went to work alone that night. I thought it was okay, because he was getting much better, but when Eddie didn't respond to something he wanted him to do right away, he punched Eddie yet again. This had not happened for a long time.

Eddie got mad, and the babysitter had to hold him back from trying to hit his dad. At that time, Eddie had just made the decision to go to West Point, and been accepted, so the babysitter said, "Eddie, don't do that. You have a bright future, okay? If you do this you're going to go to jail." Eddie didn't hit his dad back.

The babysitter called me right away, so I ran home right away, but the babysitter was so scared, she gave me notice the next day that she would be quitting by the end of the month. I said to myself, "There's no one who wants to take care of him." More accurately, I felt, there was no one who wanted to take care of me, because by that point, the babysitter wasn't taking care of him as much as cleaning and cooking for me, helping me a lot with the tasks that would otherwise be neglected because of looking after Rocky. She helped me a lot, even driving Mia around. I thought, "Now, I won't have anybody. I'll have to do all that myself."

I took comfort, when I could convince myself that any progress was being made, in one thought: "Rocky's getting better."

Rocky was left with Mia once because Eddie wasn't home, and I was working at the restaurant. Mia called me and said, "Mom, daddy tried to hit me." Okay. I just threw everything down and drove home. When I got home, Mia was scared, sitting there crying, and Rocky was acting like nothing was happening, sitting there eating his snacks like a little baby. Once a fight was over, he didn't care. I said, "Rocky, why did you do that to Mia?" Then he swore at me. I thought to myself, "How are you going to argue with him?"

Another time, Rocky wanted Mari to take him somewhere. Mari didn't respond right away, and he got so pissed off, he wanted to hit Mari, but she ran faster than him, and she managed to close the door between the kitchen and the laundry room. Well, by now, you know how strong he is. He hit the door, the door broke, and he went right through.

Every time that happened, the kids said, "Mom, you are the crazy person." I said, "Every time we find a way to resolve these situations with your dad without something bad happening, I see something improve in him. I know he can get better than this. And I don't know, if I am crazy, it's just this accident that drove me crazy, just like him."

Many things like that happened, but I didn't give up. I got very close a couple of times, like when Rocky hit Eddie, because I didn't want my kids to suffer. I was very close, but I didn't give up.

Now I know I might have been deluding myself a bit, or expecting too much of myself, not to mention the rest of the family, because it's been almost three years at the time of writing, and I can see Rocky really getting better.

Before, when I went to church, Rocky was not a believer. He always complained when I went to church, not a lot, but he didn't like it. Nevertheless, every Sunday, when we were together, I took the kids to church without him. He would go play golf, and then he would tell people I gave all the money to the church. I gave 10 percent, the 10 percent tithe that I believe is not even your money: it is God's. I don't have a problem doing that. Ten percent is God's money, not mine. When Rocky and I were together, and we went in to do the taxes, he would find out how much I gave out and tell his friends I gave all the money he made to the church.

After Rocky came back from his accident, I found a Japanese church for him. I said, "God is the only person who can help you. God is the only person who can save you. There's a Japanese church nearby, and the pastor lives five minutes from our house." He agreed to try it, so it started out that on Sunday, I would take him to his church.

He liked it, and it was so good for me. I stayed with him. He would listen to the sermon, and sing along with the congregation. I would write a check, and say, "Rocky, this is money for you to put in the offering basket." He never complained about how much it was. I said, "This is your church, so we'll split: half of our tithe will go to your church, and half to my church." Rocky would actually be happy to put in his offering, so I felt like I could say to myself, "He's changing," and sometimes he would be so moved by the sermon, I could see he was almost going to cry. I saw a change in him from going to church.

The pastor was so nice, even coming to our home to give him lessons to prepare Rocky for baptism. Rocky had come home in September 2003, and the next year, in February 2004, he got baptized.

We were all so happy. I could see joy from Mari, Eddie, and

Mia, because it was getting a little bit easier to take care of Rocky. I was starting to see smiling faces, a little bit, on everybody, something that allowed us to sit down and talk about a lot of things.

I kept learning techniques for taking care of Rocky. One thing I learned was not to get him very tired. When he got tired and hungry, he would get angry, so I would try not to let him do that. After tennis, I would bring him home, have him take a shower, and let him take a nap right away.

With everything, I had to calculate Rocky's way. I had to make him comfortable, so I felt more like his caretaker than part of a couple again, but somehow we did talk a lot. Yes, he liked to talk a lot, but I didn't have the feeling we were back together or something. I thought, "If I can go on forever taking care of him by learning new tricks, I'll be happy for that. Look on the bright side, he's taking tennis lessons, he's doing all that."

Finally, it was time for Eddie to leave for college at West Point. It's hard, the first year in West Point, so we made it into a family trip. We all drove a big van there to take Eddie. Though it was our first time driving that far we made it there and back without any major incidents.

It has now been almost four years since Rocky's accident. He now goes to church regularly and to a nursing home for care during the day. At the nursing home, we even found out that Rocky has artistic talent. In the evenings, I bring him home to be with the family. Mia especially seems to appreciate her father being home since I have to be at the restaurant.

It has not been easy, but as a family, we have found a way to get through this. And now, I feel that a new chapter of happiness has begun for our lives.

We Endure Sadness To Know Happiness

There are threads of sadness that weave their way through each generation of families. I was lucky to have broken the thread of sadness that wove its way from my mother to me. But, to be honest, much more depends on whether my break with sadness prevents Mari or Mia or Eddie from ending up in a pattern of creating self-destructive relationships.

My hope is that my acceptance of the burden to care for Rocky, after his behavior nearly destroyed our family, has laid a thread of happiness, rather than sadness, for them to follow. As I reflect on the scenes of my life, there were many signs that I was choosing to walk in the steps of my mother. Blinded by my lack of knowledge of what happiness means, I could not see that I was on the road to desperate sadness. As I close this story, I share with you the five key messages I think I have learned along the way.

Don't be afraid of your burden and don't be afraid to change.

We all have a burden to carry in life. Often we feel that the burden is too much or that it's our burden alone to carry. Many times during my struggles with Rocky I felt that way. I felt that I did not deserve the pain he was bringing to me and to our family. The shame of his actions brought an additional burden that challenged my thinking about how family life should be.

I wanted to live as I thought other families were living: Asian and American. Somehow, I wanted the best of both. But to me, Rocky could not see past what he had been in Japan. He could not see that we could have it all. In a sense, we were living two different realities without a bridge to connect them and without the words to communicate how we might build that bridge. I wanted him to change because I desired to live life differently. As I saw it, he was the one who needed to change not me!

This thinking was pervasive during most of our marriage. I thought I had to carry our burden alone, to be the one responsible, because I asked him to build this dream with me. But in truth, I never made him a partner in building our dream. For a long time, he was more like the helper than a husband or partner. Because I decided he couldn't change, I decided how things should go, and that he should just go along. This made our burdens even heavier. I never stopped building my dream long enough to understand what Rocky's dreams were. I wanted everyone to feel that they should all just be happy and thankful that I carried the burdens. I felt that they should just accept that I was making their burden lighter through all my good deeds.

Until Rocky's accident, which forced me to stop and understand his needs, I did not see what I was doing to him and others around me. His injury forced me to look at the world from his perspective, even if that world did not make sense to me. It genuinely taught me patience, and it made me see that I am not carrying my burden alone.

Throughout my struggles Li was there, my children were there, and my restaurant staff, oh my God, has been there! Without their loyalty there would be no Dee's!

I accepted and was afraid of my burden at the same time. I was afraid that I would have to do things in a different way that maybe I did not like or would not choose. I was happy for others to change but not to change myself unless I wanted to change! To genuinely accept one's burden means to go willingly without question as to how you will achieve it or why you have to achieve it.

When I first took Rocky back before the divorce, I did not accept my burden of changing my ways as a wife. I was still angry; I was still trying to create "my dream" not "our dream;" I was still thinking that I can simply take care and everyone should just be grateful. I didn't accept my burden at all, because I did not change at all!

Now I find patience and joy in taking care of Rocky, and I am thankful that he is back because I accept my burden. People say that I am crazy, but if I want my dream, I am the one who has to change. I am the one who has to change to make the family. I hope that when my kids are older, they will understand why I did this. For now, I just accept that this is what I must do.

And I can see as I change that our burdens become lighter. Rocky and I have a good relationship now. We talk. For me, it's enough that he is nice. For me, it's enough that he smiles. For me, it's enough to see the joy in his eye when he creates a new piece of art. For me, it's enough that our children want to be with their dad and that he is there for them. Through my faith in God, I have learned to not be afraid of and to accept my burden. I have learned through this experience that He will never give a burden that we cannot carry.

Don't just buy houses; build a home.

Rocky and I bought houses, but we had great difficulties creating a home. A big part of this, of course, was our upbringing. We were both from damaged families. Though we saw that the way our parents lived was not good, it seemed we were helpless to escape their fate. I became my mother and Rocky became my father. For too many years, we lived that life without realizing it. All the money we made from building the restaurant didn't change our life path. Rocky could not escape the demon of alcohol abuse, just as my father could escape the demon of drug abuse. I could not escape becoming an angry and bitter woman who wanted revenge, just as my mother could not escape the enduring bitterness she felt for my father.

Having nice homes, nice cars, and nice things didn't change any of that. Really, it enabled our behavior. Our wealth gave Rocky the license to spend as he pleased, because, like my father, he felt it was his right as the man of the house. Having suffered through building the restaurant and taking care of the children gave me license to complain, become angry, bitter, and nag Rocky because he was destroying my dream and our family. We weren't building a home. In a sense, I had created a make-believe house that looked like a home simply because it had lots of nice things it in, including a family.

My life struggles taught me how to make money but not how to build a home. I took for granted that I knew how to do this. People always liked me, and I knew how to please people so, in my mind, I knew how to build a home. I simply needed to make the family happy and take care of things. That is what I have always done: I made other people happy by taking care of things. And it seemed to work. I've learned that building a home and a family takes so much more.

I've learned that I have to understand the needs of others and address those needs, not what I think those needs are or should be. My relationship with Mari is a good example. Before, I believed that Mari should be the one to cater to my needs. When she was a baby, I needed her to go to sleep at night. When she was a toddler, I needed her to not desire and eat so many treats that her teeth became rotten. When she became a young woman, I needed her to understand my pain and take care not to upset me, as I had done for my mother. I expected all those things of Mari. Why? Because the Asian tradition says you honor your parents, it says nothing about understanding the child. I focused on what I thought was my right as a parent, not on what my daughter needed as my child.

As long as I could not see her needs, she would never honor me in the way I expected. Once I understood this, Mari came to me. Now she honors not only her parents but the family unit as well.

Rocky's injury and bringing him back into our lives forced me to see the world differently. It forced me to understand what it took to build a family. It started by understanding what the new baby in the family, Rocky, needed. In a way, I became a mother all over again. This time with the most difficult child one can imagine. In raising Rocky all over again and helping him to grow as a person, I learned how to build a family: one individual need at a time.

It's not about the American way or the Asian way

My life began, and I grew up, in the Asian ways of thinking. When I came to American, I saw other ways of thinking that I wanted to adopt for my life, notably the relationship between the husband and the wife. Through our restaurant, I have seen many different ways of cultural thinking. I adopted some of them and did not adopt others. And I can genuinely say that it has been this blending of cultures in my environment that has helped me grow so much as person.

In the restaurant, we relied on the Asian way of working together as a team with roles that are defined yet changeable. Because the staff held things together even when Rocky was not taking care of the business, we did not go totally down. I am very thankful to them for this. Without their devotion to the business, there would have been no Dee's to rebuild. For twenty-four years, they have carried the burden and legacy of Dee's with me. Yes, I am the face to the customer, but they are the body and soul that keeps the heart of the business running.

At home, we mixed the American way with the Asian way. Often, this caused problems, particularly for Rocky and me. We each adopted the parts of the American way that suited us individually without considering how it affected us jointly. This was obvious when I began to project onto Rocky my desire for him to be more like the American husbands I saw coming into my restaurant and living in our neighborhoods. While it was not wrong for me to want those things, it was culturally and personally insensitive of me to assume that Rocky could just somehow change to the person I wanted him to become. The right way for us was not Asian or American; it was the way that worked for us as a couple, not individually.

As I decided we needed to be more "American" in some ways, I never considered how we could work together as a couple to get there. The only tool I knew was to nag as my mother had done. It was obvious, from watching my mother and father as I grew older, that this tool didn't work, but I never considered trying another way. This is the problem of being stuck in one-way of doing things, culturally or otherwise. There is no American way or Asian way. There are many ways. The more open we are to accepting the possibilities of achieving what we want in different ways, the greater our chances of making those desires a reality. Rocky has taught me this.

Why I could see this in my restaurant but not apply it to the rest of my life is a mystery to me. But again, learning to take care of Rocky forced me to look for lessons in every part of my life. It has also given me the patience to find the solution. So I am very thankful that he is back helping me to see the many different ways to achieve happiness.

It's okay to fall down; it's only failure when you don't get back up.

There were many times when I lost face during the downfall of my and Rocky's marriage. I also took away Rocky's face, which is very important for Asian men. We both felt ashamed in our acceptance that we had failed our families, our community, and ourselves. At one point, my shame was so great that I wanted to kill Rocky, his girlfriend, and myself. During those times, I saw no way to get back up. I saw no way to save face. Obviously, I could not have been more wrong!

When I was choosing to not get back up, I was clearly failing. I accepted an end without seeing the possibility of a new beginning. There is no true end, not even death. If I am carrying my burden and contributing to enriching the lives we lead, this legacy will continue on long after I am gone. How arrogant was I to think that by simply disappearing from this life that my suffering will end!

My suffering would have continued in those that I touched by my words and my deeds. My suffering would have continued in the niece or nephew, son or daughter, who when faced with the same difficulties in life, had decided to follow my path to death. My suffering would have continued in the friends, family, restaurant staff, and customers who would miss my smiles and caring deeds. My suffering would have continued in the Asian community who would miss my contribution as a neighbor, business owner, civic leader, mother, friend, and the myriad of other roles I played in my daily life.

When I choose to not get back up, I choose to say I can't and won't learn to live life differently. Accepting failure by definition meant that I could not learn, I could not improve, I should not make mistakes, and somehow I should always be perfect. None of which, of course, is realistic or desirable. We have to fail, because we have a need to continuously learn. Without learning there really is no point to being here.

Through the failure of my marriage, one important lesson that I learned was to not back people into a corner. I backed Rocky into a corner. When I backed him into the corner, I gave him no way to return to the family. One message that I want women who are going through difficult relationships to learn from my experience is to give your husband, boyfriend, or significant other a way to return to the relationship. Everyone makes mistakes. Give people an opportunity to see their mistakes and to correct them. Do not push your loved ones or anyone, for that matter, into a corner.

Value the people and things that bring you happiness along life's journey.

There were many times during our marriage that I did not value Rocky. I didn't value his hard work during the early years of our marriage. All I could see was that he slept a lot. I did not value the things he enjoyed like going to see the Ali boxing movie or playing golf. All I could see was fighting on the screen and time spent away from the kids and me. I didn't value his contribution to the restaurant. All I could see was that he didn't do it the way that I would do it, as if there were only one way to get it right! I guess I had contempt for Rocky and did not know it.

This contempt led me to believe that my way was the only way it should be. It led me to tolerate but not accept or understand Rocky's way of thinking or doing things.

At times, I was so blinded by what I thought I alone brought to the marriage that I could not see the small ways that he valued me. And Rocky did value me, even though he could not easily show it! Very early on in our relationship, I lost sight of the small ways he valued me. I also lost sight of the fact that we should enjoy the fruit of our hard work. Even in his brain-damaged condition, Rocky could see that I did not value this. He said: "My wife doesn't know how to have fun. She's too hardworking."

I have learned to value Rocky and the contribution he makes to our lives. When Rocky is at the restaurant and tries to seat customers, I value that, even if he swears. When Rocky brings me little Mochis as a treat, I value that. When he has patience, I value that. Not only do I value it, but also I receive great happiness from it. Really, I cannot and should not ask for more.

Sometimes, we endure great sadness and pain to force us to see things differently. I have learned to accept and address the threads of sadness that ran through the lives of my family. By having the will to change, I can see a better future for my family. I attribute this to my strong belief in God. When I was young, I went to church because it was better than being at home. As a young adult, I left the church completely. I returned to the church in 1986 and have been committed to a life of serving God since that time. His blessings have made these changes possible. I hope that by sharing my story that this will help your family, too.

So now, you know, what was going on in my personal life behind the smiles you might have grown accustomed to seeing, the smiles that hid the sadness. Now, behind the smiles, you can picture me as the wiser woman I have become. I think the sadness has gone. Now, behind the smiles, I have faith, and I have questions, plus a lifetime of memories and warm thoughts about the people who are part of the community around Dee's Restaurant. I now know how blessed, lucky, and fortunate, I really am. Now when I cry, I'm crying tears of joy and that, of course, no matter what is going on is now why I smile!

Photographs

The Kang family back together.
From left to right, standing: Mia, Eddie, and Mari
Seated: Robert and Dee

This is my baby picture taken when I was one year old.

Rocky's mother (front) before her death in Japan with an unidentified woman.

My mother and father.

My sister, youngest brother, and me at home in Korea.

My graduation day from junior high.

My brothers (stripe shirts), a friend, and me.

This is me (on the right) with friends from school.

My first year in Japan.

This is the teddy bear that Rocky gave me as a gift during the early days of our courtship.

Rocky when he was a Yakuza in Osaka, Japan.

Rocky and me when we first arrived in America and had bought our first car, a Chevy Camaro.

Rocky as a sushi chef at the Japanese Steak House.

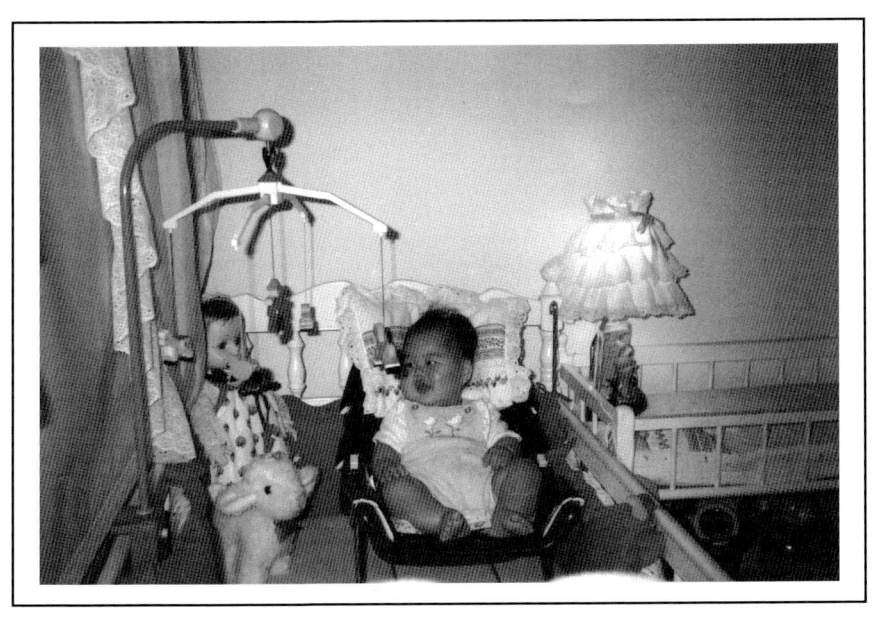

Mari in her crib surrounded by toys and furnishings that I purchased at garage sales.

Mari and Eddie playing in the yard at the house in Glencoe, IL.

My mother and father at his 71st birthday celebration.

Rocky, Mari, and me at my father's 71st birthday celebration.

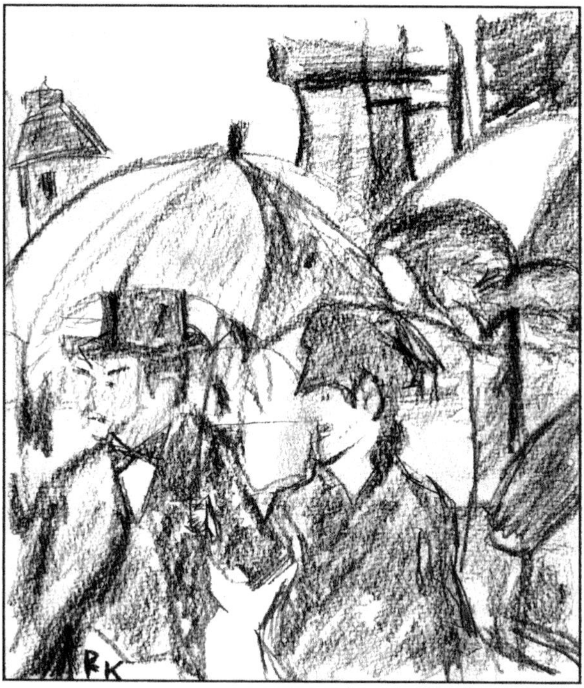
RK

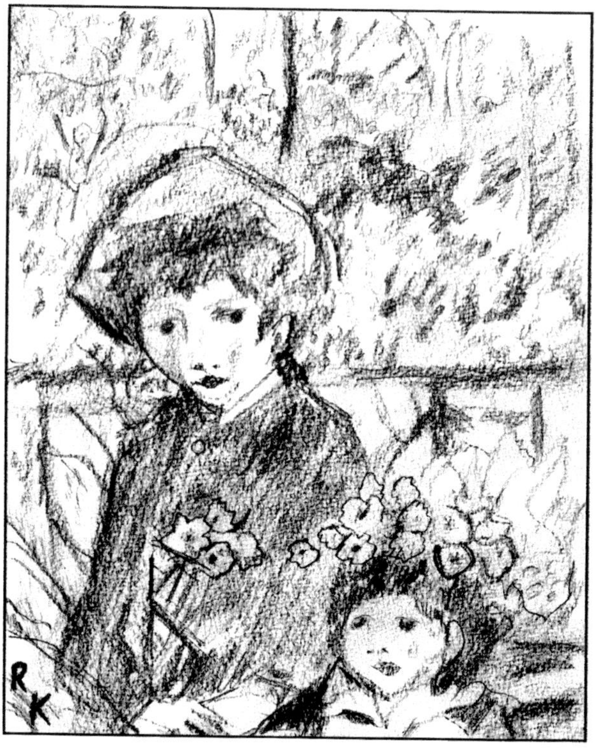
RK

Rocky gets therapeutic care during the day at the House of Welcome North Shore Senior Center. During his drawing classes, we found that he has natural artistic talent. Here are some of the drawings he has done.

Rocky getting baptized in September, 2004.

My baptism in October, 1986.

My mother and oldest brother

The family on a cruise to the Bahamas after we learned that my father has cancer.

Li and me in May, 2006 at the Hudson River visiting Eddie at West Point.

Mari and me at the finisher's line after the Chicago Marathon in October, 2006.